DREAM

M000308877

Awaken your Life's Destiny

Jennifer Brooke Partridge

Mica ♥
Your brilliance
is a creative gift to
the world ~ share it, shine it
LIVE IT !!! ... I Believe in YOU !!!...

All my love ~
Jen xox

Dream Awake

Copyright © 2011 by Jennifer Brooke Partridge

ISBN: 978-0-9893555-0-6

Second Edition: California, USA

Disclaimer

The author and publisher of this book are not responsible in any manner whatsoever for any injury that may occur through following the instructions contained herein. It is recommended that before beginning the techniques, you consult with your physician to determine whether you are medically, physically and mentally fit to undertake this course of practice.

Artwork completed by: Chris Jackson & Justin Totemical.
www. totemical.com/

Published by
Our New Earth
P.O. Box 382, Ojai,
California, USA, 93024
Email: info@ournewearth.tv
Website: www.ournewearth.tv

In dedication, and special thanks to my dearest friend Amaya for his support through the creation of this book, may your heart continue to shine!

Table of Contents

Chapter 1

Consciousness into Duality

Consciousness

The birth of pure consciousness is based on a deep feeling of emptiness when there is no thought. Everything that appears after the space of no thought is the illusion or the dream, for anything that contains something is a projection, thus creating an identity and this is how the dream was born.

We are about to take a journey into a world that strips the layers away from who you think you are. This is a timely experience for you, since life for all beings on the Earth seems to be getting more complicated by the day. Every year seems to fly by faster than the year before and the memories of this life appear to be jumbled into one big experience. A lot of the time we are so bombarded with experiences that we find it hard to take time out to experience the clarity and wisdom in these moments. Along with all these new experiences by the day, the world around us seems to mirror its growth with the continual development in new technologies, gadgets, and communication devices. Combining all these together, I guess you could say, "life has become busier than ever". With this said, we as a species are finding that we can cram more into a day than ever before and this could mean more money, more profit, more spending, more connecting, more growing, more sharing, more evolution, and more dreaming.

That's why I decided to write this book – so that you may take time out and find perspective on your life while recognizing the power of your dream. But before we dive right into the nitty gritty of dreamtime, I think we should start at the beginning and I mean literally the beginning. Before time existed and before you were even a twinkle in the universe's eye. The reason why it's important to start from the beginning is so that you can see how fast things can grow and where we've come from in order to be the master of creating your dream reality in the now.

There are many ancient civilizations that point to the birth of a new age or consciousness, from the great Mayans, to the Hopi People, Ancient Egyptians, Australian Aboriginals, Indians, to almost every native group birthed in ancient history. All these systems of thought pointed to a date of around December 21st, 2012 where they say one world state of consciousness shall shift into a new dimension. Many of these ancient texts and teachings were misread and calculated in the wrong manner, spreading fearful ideas to humanity and professing the end of the world. What I propose to do in this book is to inspire you to see your reflection through this prophecy of "the end of the world" and see how in many ways you're also moving from one world to the next. With every door that closes a new one shall be opened and this is our opportunity today.

Throughout history we can see that we've passed through many eras and many ways of expressing life. From the times of hunters and gatherers all the way to a consumerist world, hungry for not only nuts and berries, but also technology and cars and the world of things. As the world continues to grow, more and more "things" are in demand. So what do we do with all these demands?

In the beginning

Take a breath and become aware of the oxygen moving through your body, expanding your diaphragm and then releasing through your lungs, notice the moment between the breath in and the breath out. We like to call this the still point; it is the moment between moments where nothing is happening – the moment before a change in direction. However, before the still point occurred (between breaths) there was plenty of action. The airways were filling up your lungs, oxygen was moving through your body fueling your blood with life substance and then for a small moment nothing. This was then shortly followed by an outward breath and the release of carbon dioxide back into the environment around you. Then the contracting of your lungs as they prepared for another breath.

Many of the ancient texts throughout history, such as the Vedic texts from India, will share the same knowledge that I'm here sharing with you today. I hope to place the context of this knowledge in a new way for you to perceive. The intention is that you gain a physical understanding on how this information can affect your life. As I refer to the still point between breaths I hope you feel, if only for a moment, where pure consciousness lives. The void between acting and doing – the moment of nothing before conscious action takes place. Take a few more breaths and become aware of that moment between the, inhale and the, exhale, that small moment before the change in direction.

As you become aware of the moment between breaths, you're becoming aware of pure consciousness from which everything is first birthed. This is the moment of oneness – the merging of all energies together and the awareness of itself as one. During the process of action and movement, it's easy to forget that everything is unified. This is due to us becoming the action rather than watching the action unfold. By allowing ourselves to practice awareness in every moment of our lives we're able to weave doing and being together.

For a moment, let's reflect on your day. In your mind, let's play a movie on what has occurred so far:
- What are you wearing today?
- What was the process you used to choose your clothes?
- How many conversations have you had today?
- What was the highlight of your day so far?
- What was the first thing you did when you opened your eyes this morning?
- What food or drink have you eaten today?
- How many phone calls have you made today?

There are many more questions I could ask which would propel you into the memories of your day but I believe these six simple questions are suffice to paint a picture of the busy-ness in your life. During these activities, how many times were you aware of your breath? Or even better, how many times during these activities were you aware of the zero point between your breaths.

It's not easy to remain this aware in all of our activities because our mind has a tendency to be occupied in the doing rather than the simple being as mentioned previously.

As I take you back to the beginning of time, before you, our planet, the galaxy, or even the universe and all its stars existed, right back to the zero point. This is the point of nothingness from where everything was formed – the void from which everything emerged. So how did everything in the universe get created out of nothing?

When you have an idea or a dream to create something in your life, perhaps a vision for a new job, or to create a painting, or to run that marathon, where did this vision first begin? It always begins from nothingness and is birthed through a thought in your mind.

This is the same mechanics for the continual creation in the greater universe. In the beginning it was a lot easier because there were not a whole lot of other thoughts to influence the new ones. In our day and age, our universe appears a lot more complex with a lot more thoughts flying around, which ultimately influences our vision in a greater way. But in the beginning, there was simply nothing. So the first ingredient in the universe would have been more abstract than our complex and structured viewpoint of our current reality.

So image now that there is nothing – just awareness, oneness, and then this awareness became aware that it was aware. This would then make two points of consciousness rather than just one. Now you would have:

- The awareness (pure consciousness or absolute reality)
  plus
- The awareness that you are aware (projection upon reality)

$(1 + 1 = 2)$ When this equation takes place, duality is born and this will keep growing as more projections upon reality continue. Many ancient cultures will point to this same understanding, however a common ingredient in all ancient cultures is that they often use metaphors and symbols to tell the story of creation. In many ways this is a better way to communicate the truth, because story's are usually a lot easier to remember and much more practical to be passed down to any generation or person of learning capacity. For example in Vedic knowledge, they tell this story through Shiva and Shakti, the birth of two polar opposite energies, the masculine and feminine. You can also see this in Christianity through the story of Adam and Eve. Also it is interesting to note that in the story of Adam and Eve, upon eating the forbidden fruit they are expelled from the Garden of Eden. The fruit in this case represents the "knowledge" of good and evil, which is the birth of separation consciousness, which we will talk about shortly.

Now, jumping back to our practical understanding of these metaphors and the birth of creation. When you look at the watch on your wrist and your mind tells you that it is in fact a watch. It was the awareness that see's the watch and the thought in your mind that labeled it a watch. Yet, in truth if your consciousness wanted to break it down further, it could then label it in parts, such as the numbers, shapes, the type of material, etc. It could even go one step further and simply perceive it as vibrating energy that only appears to be solid to the eye, which perceives solid matter. So in reality, your mind perceives what it has been trained to perceive.

Now as we go back to the first ever thought birthed in the universe, we can see that there are two things that exist in the universe – the awareness and the projection (or the label) of what you believe the awareness to be. This is when identity comes into play. Pure consciousness is playing a game of hide and seek as it places ideas of what it "thinks" the ultimate reality to be. This game will then continue to grow until more and more labels upon labels will be born, eventually creating the world and the universe we live in with all the complexities, stories, systems of thought, mechanics of nature and the science of everything that we experience on a day to day basis.

- The awareness
- The awareness of the awareness
- The awareness of the awareness of 2
- The awareness of the awareness of 1 and 2 and 3 and so on...

Now imagine that over the whole span of creation, more and more projections have taken place, creating more ideas of what reality is and thus forming the dream in which we live in. Now imagine the eons of time that have existed prior to this point in awareness. That is the depth of our dream.

Pure Consciousness

As you can see, everything was born from a place of pure consciousness, which is the unification of all – many people refer to this as oneness or pure awareness. It's only due to the continual process of projecting upon the pure consciousness that life appears separate and we have forgotten our simple truth of unity. The plus to this moment in time is that we are now re-remembering and are once again capable of grasping a level of understanding that we truly are unified by all things. This means we can start developing some tools to benefit from this knowledge. For those who are reading this book and also individuals coming from a scientific stand point in perceiving reality, I'm sure by breaking everything down into energy frequency you'll see that everything is one, just vibrating at different rates. For example, everything from the chair you're sitting in, the book you're holding, to the plants outside, and even the water that you drink are all vibration. The denser forms of vibrations such as this book and the chair are just vibrating at a slower rate than air and water. All elements in our reality are vibrating energy, that holds information. They are all connected by energy and unified into one field. The denser forms are more visible to the physical eye and the light frequencies are less physically available to the eye. However, as we move into greater connectedness to the oneness, our perception of all these unified realities begin to merge and you can switch your perception to any mode you wish. This is one of the great benefits to developing these tools.

When the field of perception is cleaned, we are able to step into remembering our oneness to all things. This moment of recognition is the moment when you realize that this connection to oneness was here all along and it was only your mind that was disconnecting you. We all have moments in our life of feeling unity. Perhaps you're watching a sunset or holding your lovers hand as you walk along the beach. Maybe smelling the fresh fragrance of a frangipani flower or receiving a compliment from your boss at work for a job well done. Whatever the situation, I'm sure you can reflect upon a time when you felt that moment of connection and unity. For some people, these feelings are fleeting and far and few between. While other people seem to celebrate in the field of unity all the time. So what makes some people more capable of feeling unity than others? The answer is awareness. As we do practices that bring us into awareness, we find that we are able to remember this unity along the path of life more frequently. For their could be two people standing with their feet sunk into the sand on a tropical island, watching the sunset turn into bright oranges across the distant sky, yet the perception of reality in both parties could be completely different. Perhaps person 1 has had a busy day and they're in conflict with their wife/husband about whose turn it is to cook dinner. Person 2 has come to the beach already in a peaceful state, with little thought bothering them. The person with little thought bothering them is able to access the awareness of life's beauty a lot easier than the person who is carrying around conflict. So every day, ask yourself, "What am I carrying around that no longer serves me?" This one question alone will help you become aware of the elements in your life that you wish to let go of. The first step is becoming aware of that and the second step is letting go!

Oneness Exercise

The following exercise is one of the many great tools you'll receive in this book that will allow you to connect to greater levels of oneness, which exist inside of you. The benefits can be huge if you commit to developing these intuitive abilities throughout your life. Read through this exercise once and then put it into practice.

Close your eyes and become aware of your body. How does it feel? What sensations are orchestrating within your body? Are there areas of tightness, heaviness, and lightness, buzzing frequencies, discomfort?

Now focus on any areas within your body that may feel more prominent. Perhaps there's a buzzing feeling in your stomach or a tingling in your leg or you feel stress in your shoulders? Take a breath and imagine that you are breathing oxygen into that area of your body. Hold your breath for 5 seconds and then as you slowly release the breath, feel that area of your body expand and release energy into the outer area of your energetic body (some traditions call this your aura). This is the non-physical part of your body. Now tune into that area just outside your body and feel the connection of energy outside to the physical connection inside of your body. If you want to use this exercise as a healing exercise you can choose to keep breathing oxygen in to those areas of discomfort and then releasing the breath after 5 seconds. As you continue to do this, you will feel your energy field start to expand and no longer are you simply aware of your physical body, you're becoming aware of your energy body, which connects to the non-physical and all things in your environment. Many of these spiritual technologies were developed a long time before modern science and can be found across the board in ancient traditions around the planet. It is documented that for over 5000 years the sacred sages and yogis of India and Tibet taught many breathing and physical exercises to purify the body and mind. This was taught with the intention to unify the person with the awareness of ultimate reality.

In today's world, people have become so swept away with acting and reacting that they have forgotten these simple tools of awareness. This can be very hazardous for an individual because the moment they feel a discomfort in their body, they turn to drugs and other distractions that only works at shutting down the awareness of the problem instead of becoming aware of it and healing themselves through the root cause. In these instances of escapism, the problem doesn't go away. Only the awareness that the problem is there goes away. For example, when you have a headache, this is your body's natural way of telling you to place awareness on that part of your body. That way you can heal yourself. Perhaps it's telling you that your mind is working too hard and needs a rest? Maybe you need more water to hydrate your brain or a number of other reasons? The point is that instead of allowing your awareness to guide you to a solution, you pop a pill and shut off your awareness all together. Over time, not only will your headaches get worse, but this may also mean more drugs in your system. This ultimately leads to more physical imbalance in your body and forces your organs of elimination to work harder to detoxify your system. Not to mention all of the other ailments developing in your body from the build up of these hazardous substances.

The Birth of Duality

Prescription drugs are just one example of a coping mechanism that we as a species have implemented into our life to deal with discomfort in our energy field. I believe a coping mechanism is a system that was developed within the human psyche to switch of the awareness of a problem. The reason why human beings develop this system is because there has not been the proper education to connect people to their true nature – which is unity consciousness. Instead, we keep creating layers upon layers to deal with the projections and complications created from the illusions in the mind. This propels us into further states of separation and disconnection from our environment and the people around us.

It is our individual thoughts that create our disconnection from unity. This is because we as individuals start to believe that we're responsible for our lives, in such a way that it becomes me verses them. This me verses them syndrome is also a defense mechanism based on the illusion of separation. When we are in this state of consciousness, we tend to behave in ways that don't honor the sacredness and unity of all things. You only have to scan the world to see the amount of wars, lies, and deceit that occur in people's consciousness, separating them from the truth. People will kill, steal, and cheat to survive in this world because they have been trained to believe that it is the only way to survive and if they don't behave in these ways, their life will be in danger.

Competition

Duality brings about the fight or flight mentality, which makes individuals move into a competitive mode. You can easily see this on a global scale as countries fight for resources, oil, and other wealth buried in the sands of their distant neighbors. More close to home, you can see this on the corner of the street as shops compete against each other to sell the most toys – or when kids fight over the last candy cane. Wherever you see this type of competition, you can almost be certain that duality is at play.

Competition can be a friendly sport but it has turned into an instinct of survival – a survival of the egos. Everyone in their time has met a healthy athlete who plays the game for fun and I'm sure everyone has also met an athlete who plays the game to win and knock out all of his competitors. There's a distinct difference between the two. The healthy example always remembers his/her connection to unity, which allows the game to be fun. The unhealthy example feels threatened by the other and feels they need to pull every move necessary to survive and kill the competition.

Light and Dark

The moment that awareness of awareness was born was the moment that light and dark came into existence. No longer was there just one, but now two. This then creates two opposing forces in the field of awareness. The first: being the awareness and the unification and knowingness of its true nature. The second: being the projection of who it believes it "self" to be, which is usually disconnected from absolute truth (oneness). Every perception made, is only one possibility of infinite possibilities in the field of awareness. Some may say that the ego is the dark and the knowingness is the light. The ego is separated from unification and as a result, will always try to prove itself to be correct and will do whatever it takes to be right. The reason for this is anything that is unconscious of its true self (oneness), will contain fear and anything that is in fear will do what ever it takes to protect itself in order to survive.

Chapter 2

Duality Creates Illusion

Projecting the Illusion

As mentioned in the previous chapter, the world that we currently live in with all of its hustle and bustle is mostly made up of projections. To sum it all up, there are many pros for this great big projection but like all things, there are also cons. The pros are that we get to create a world together that is based on agreement. Whatever the collective world agrees to, becomes a fact in the world of illusion or the world of perceived reality!

For example, as a member of the human species we have developed many amazing systems that benefit the greater population, such as our general survival means like the food we eat, the water we drink, the sustainable technologies, the houses we live in, and the utensils we cook with. We've also developed languages, art, culture, self-expression, and other beautiful gifts that bring joy to this world. All of these developments have become second nature to our survival and a part of the effortless flow we are capable of creating in this life. I believe all of these expressions have come from a space of unity with all things. Any great invention will take into mind not only how it affects the individual but the world at large. This is unity consciousness.

When something is created in the field that works selfishly, then it most likely comes from a place of the ego. The reason is that the ego fears survival. Therefore, it wishes to make a quick fix to its reality or it fears it will die. This "quick fix" mentality can create an array of hazardous challenges for our agreed upon reality. Many of these poor decisions, will create the degeneration of the Earth and its natural resources. Yet ultimately all bad decisions will lead us into a "wake up" call, which will once again return us to a state of oneness. For example, we are now seeing the challenges of global warming, war, and famine occurring through out the world. The reason why these stories are taking place is because the majority of the people involved in these challenges have agreed on the illusion, as passed down from generation to generation, and as a result the illusion exists. It is very hard for an individual to wake up from the illusion when they have been taught through their whole life that the illusion is real and the people that taught them this fact were the same children who learned it from their parents.

When we place trust in another person's reality, we are agreeing to their projected idea of reality. This is not always a bad thing if the person you are relying on is connected to unity consciousness. But most of the time this is not the case. They are usually connected to what they learned or read somewhere and now they are passing it on to you. That's why it is important to stop relying on the projections around you and get in touch with yourself. By getting to know yourself and pulling off all the layers of everything you have been taught, you are able to access unity consciousness. Peeling off the layers of illusion is nothing to be afraid of because in attaining this place of unity, everyone benefits. It is inclusive of all things and comes from a space of love.

Love

Think back to a time in your life when you felt great waves of love move through your being. Maybe you were falling in love for the first time? Perhaps you were noticing the beauty in your partner's eyes as they read poetry to you? Maybe it was when your parents tucked you into bed at night as a child, or your best friend called just to say how much they appreciate you? All these feelings are examples of love and create feelings of unity. When we are in a true state of love, there's an unconditional energy that becomes greater than your ego. It is an energy that puts the other before you. Some examples of unconditional love would be when your mom spends her last dollar on getting you that jacket you want – or when you fully accept your partner for whom they are regardless of their faults. This unconditional love is a part of unity consciousness; there fore you can never be let down. You are able to see that everything is always working for the growth of all individuals. The only time love lets you down is when it was never love in the first place. Rather, it was another emotion such as attachment masquerading as love. The best way to tell if it is really love is to ask your self this question; if I lose this relationship, am I able to be unconditional? When you're able to move into this unconditional state, you're able to step into a greater flow of life, recognizing that everything is transitory. Greater depths of compassion are able to develop and the wisdom is recognized that all is working for the enfoldment of true reality and knowingness of self. Although there may be pain on the surface in many situations, there's a true knowingness that all perceived pain is pointing to clarity and guiding the individual to remember who they are. Unfortunately, pain must often be felt in order for individuals to grow in their ability to appreciate life, love deeper, and honor and respect them selves, which are all elements of unity consciousness.

When we are in a true state of love, there is no need to place false projections upon reality. It's only when we are in a state of fear that false projections begin to raise their ugly head. For example, in your early days of falling in love, you had a partner who cheated and lied to you. This caused your ego a lot of pain because you were attached to wanting their love in a certain way. Since you didn't get what you wanted, you created pain in your body. As a result, from that moment forward every relationship that you experience you start to see through the lenses of pain. Maybe you accuse your new partner of cheating on you? Or you start arguments based on the fact that you believe they are lying to you? All of these projections that you are creating in your mind are due to the fact that when you first picked up those beliefs you were not connected to unconditional love.

When we try to put demands on people in our life, we are creating conditions for our love. This is a process of the ego, which is separate from a space of truly knowing yourself as oneness. These demands that we place on people usually have to do with areas in our life where we feel insecure. These insecurities are also coming from a place of not knowing yourself. Therefore, you're hoping to find yourself through the other. When the other person does not deliver your expectations, more pain is created in your psyche and within the physical body temple. This in turn propels you further into the mode of separation. Any time you might be experiencing these feelings of separation, all you have to do is move yourself into awareness, feel your body, notice your thoughts, and move into forgiveness. These steps will guide you into surrendering your attachment to a desired outcome and will set you free into truly being the awareness of unity that you are.

Thoughts create a dream state

As you can see, the process of thoughts and perception are what create the illusion in your day-to-day life. The more thoughts you have, the more you are usually lost in the illusion of what you believe to be real. As I mentioned before, it's not always so bad to be playing in the illusion. After all, we are human and part of our experience is to play this game. The game can be a lot of fun, especially if you have managed to create a world based on abundance, joy, celebration, and all of those other great feelings and experiences one desires. People who have a tendency of losing themselves in the illusion completely, often swing on almighty highs and almighty lows. The reason for this is that it can be easy to lose your center if you have forgotten the greater truth, which is; your awareness of unity even in the happiest of days. For example, you may find out that you have just won the lotto and it was a one million dollar jackpot. You are ecstatic and over the moon when you go to cash the winning ticket in. Then you find out that 100 other people also had the lucky numbers you chose, so the money has to be split between 100 people. In response, your high held swing then plummets back into a low one. As you can see, this is an example of conditional love. You were only happy because of the conditions and then when the conditions changed, your state of happiness changed.

All of these thoughts that go through our mind on a day-to-day basis can be seen as a dream state from which our consciousness is continually projecting images onto our canvas of life and telling us stories. For those of you who have ever studied dream interpretation, you'll see that as we close our eyes at night we also go into a dream. This dream state is usually a lot more unconscious than our waking dream state. Yet all are the same. They are both levels of dreamtime because they are based on the reality that our level of consciousness is painting.

Now let's discuss the type of dream state we go into when we sleep at night. Some people are more fortunate than others and remember their dreams. They are usually recalled within the first few moments of opening your eyes. This is due to being in between states of consciousness. When this occurs you are still partially in the other state of consciousness while you are merging into your waking consciousness. This allows your waking consciousness to recall the other state and the messages received in your other reality.

Regardless of what type of dream you are experiencing, you're consciousness is continually being fed symbols to decode your reality. When we are aware of what these symbols in our dreams mean, we have a road map to understand ourselves. On the other hand, if we are unable to read the symbols, then navigating our reality can be a lot more complex and challenging.

Consciousness Projects Symbols

The truth is even if you are totally lost in the illusion of your reality and life seems to be a nightmare, (perhaps you just lost your job, you have a serious illness or your boyfriend/girlfriend just left you) you still have contact to the pure consciousness within yourself. Your pure consciousness is the space that knows and is aware of everything. Pure consciousness is fed into your reality through symbols and images, so that you can wake up and remember your unity once more. This is why you can never be completely lost in your dream. There will always be signposts to guide you through. The only question is, how aware are you of the signposts in your life? If you don't know how to tune into the symbols around you, life can be like walking through a foreign country and all you see are road signs written in different languages and symbols – you have no idea what they mean. So in this instance, what would you do? Perhaps you find someone who speaks your language and hopefully they can point you in the right direction. Or maybe that person knows someone else who can point you in the right direction? Either way, our natural human instincts will find a way.

Using the example above; when you have very little awareness of the signs and symbols, you are forced to rely on people along the way to point you in the right direction. But perhaps you decide to move to a foreign country and study their language for a year. After a year of living in this new country, you may be reading all the road signs, talking their language and probably even driving their cars!

This is the same process that we go through as we learn to navigate our internal reality. As we learn the tools and techniques needed to be self aware, we become more in tune with reading the symbols and following the sign posts given to us in our life.

Consider these signposts as spiritual guidance. They are not completely the same as road signs in a foreign country. The difference is that these signs come from our soul and the pure awareness of what is guiding our soul in to greater understanding and mastery for our life.

Awareness of the Signs

Signs can come in many different forms and are usually encoded into the illusion of your dream so that your current state of consciousness can understand it. As you become more aware of the signs, you start to notice them everywhere. Your life can transfer from being totally lost in the dream to being blissfully guided in each and every moment by the abundance of signposts. Here is a short list of potential signposts that may be showing up in your world every day. Are there any additional signposts you can add?

- An unexpected phone call.
- Something that someone mentions to you.
- A book lands on your desk at work and it's just what you needed to read.
- You hear a song in the car containing a message.
- You miss the exit on the freeway and are guided a different way home, beating the traffic that was once ahead of you.
- You lose your job, only to find a new and better job one month later.
- All of a sudden, you keep bumping into a person out of the blue and you later realize that there's some business that you can do together.

More Abstract Signposts:

- A symbol such as a type of animal with certain qualities shows up in certain places.
- You keep being drawn to a specific color and you realize that this color vibration works with a specific emotion.
- When you are doodling on a piece of paper you start to draw specific shapes. Each shape holds a different quality that represents qualities of your consciousness; some are more masculine or feminine while others directly relate to different systems of information.
- Different smells remind you of a loved one that has passed, and perhaps you realize that they are trying to send you a message.

As you become aware that everything moving through your reality is moving for your benefit, then you start to see opportunities everywhere. This is part of the advantage of being in touch with the higher laws of the universe.

In the process of breaking down the illusion, your ability to see new perspectives in your waking life become more expansive, whereas before you were only able to perceive a certain situation or person in one light. Perhaps you always had an opinion that the girl down the street from you is a bimbo. Then one day you broke down your critical perception of her and decided to talk to her only to realize that she is a human just like you and with that comes her own insecurities, but most importantly love. Through opening up to this new level of communication with her, you were able to see that your opinion of her was just created through the projections in your mind.

As we open our mind wider to new realities, we are able to understand the symbols placed in our world. We have been taught for a very long time that it is wrong to think abstractly and that the world is meant to be linear. This belief stops us from seeing the infinite possibilities that are available to us every day. Then an extraordinary individual comes along who only sees life through abstract goggles and we think that they are insane or handicapped. But the truth is that many of the most amazing geniuses in the world were thought to be insane. Many of them had trouble living in our linear reality but they were able to bring through profound wisdom that shifted our consciousness forever.

The truth is, as we open ourselves to see not only through linear eyes but also through entertaining abstract concepts, we as a consciousness are able to grow. Therefore our life is able to become more expansive. In approaching this, we become liberated and realize that there is no right or wrong, just right or left. Everything is exactly the way it is meant to be. All realities no matter how abstract they may appear are actually capable of living in harmony together. It is only when one reality tries to impose itself on another reality that challenges arise. That is is why I've learned through my life that even if you believe you have the solution to someone's problem; don't give it to him or her unless they ask for it.

When someone approaches you with a question, they are more open to receiving the answer because they asked for it. If someone does not ask the question, then they are most likely still going through their own internal process, trying to figure it out through their own paradigm. Once they have exhausted all areas of searching through their paradigm, they may ask you for a perspective. By allowing others to go through their own process, you are letting them know that you trust their process, regardless of the result. In response to your supportive nature, they feel trust in the same way, and are open to seeing your viewpoint.

Abstract signposts

As mentioned above, our consciousness will find the sign posts from which it mostly relates to in its current state of consciousness. It will work through your filters to deliver you messages of insight to your life's challenges and guide you in directions of greater health, wellness, prosperity, and success (if you let it!). When we open ourselves to see the viewpoints of people around us, we free our mind of the cobwebs. Some viewpoints may resonate with us, while others may make us giggle. Yet when we are free (in our mind) to realize that all viewpoints are valid, then we no longer try to prove our viewpoint. We simply live it in accordance to the benefits it creates in our life.

Now imagine for the first time your mind is open and free. You are not trying to prove nor are you trying to defend anything. You are in a space of allowing everything to be as it is. How does that feel? I can tell you it's a weight off my shoulders! Take a moment just to feel this new level of openness – nothing to prove and nothing to defend; simply allowing! What does your mind feel like in this state? How are you viewing your relationships? How do you see those around you?

You can take this simple practice out into your life. Whenever you feel there is a conflict between yourself and another individual, try taking this standpoint.: Nothing to prove, nothing to defend. The reason why people will often dive into a full-blown argument is because they fear if their viewpoint is proven incorrect, they will have no identity and will no longer know themselves. But if we always remember that the thoughts and the illusions are not our true identity, then we are free to play in the games we wish and let go of the games that no longer serve our purpose.

All of the illusions of the mind are simply layers throughout our pure consciousness. Let's not forget that we are always unified to all things. This new spaciousness of mind will open you up to greater heights of perceiving the signs around you and will allow you to work with the messages of the universe in a greater way for the greater service to yourself, humanity, the planet, and ultimately, the intelligence of the whole universe.

The universe is an illusion

Now that we are surrendering all of our viewpoints on reality, I'm going to play a little game with you and take you into another realm of reality – The Universe!

In today's world, we only have to switch on the Discovery Channel to watch the latest updates in the developing universe. We can retrieve information on the planets that orbit our galaxy. We can sense the sound vibrations of the sun, all the way into distant and far away star systems and galaxies in the farther reaches of our universe. There is a strong interest in the developing universe and every day there seems to be new discoveries and revelations as to what the universe is and what it holds. The way we calculate our answers is through the technologies we have developed and the definitions we give to these certain calculations. These calculations are of course based on the reality of what we have labeled to be true and what we can see through the human eye and our developed awareness as a species. But what if Einstein was right when he said we only use 10% of our brain at most? Would that mean we are not fully seeing the equation as it truly is? Are we filtering our 90% of what is actually present on the surface? What would happen if when we looked through a telescope (or even a microscope) and saw with 100% of our full awareness? Would the picture look different?

It was not long ago that people thought the Earth was flat, yet in order for the world to change, it took new eyes to see that the Earth was not flat. It took a daring sailor to continue sailing into the horizon, outside of his comfort zone, to recognize that the horizon continues all the way around the Earth. We are waking up in to new ways of seeing every day? That is why I inspire you to look differently at the information you receive and instead, acknowledge it as a viewpoint and not reality.

The human mind has created itself in the land of projections and things, so naturally it wants to place labels on what it believes the natural universe to be, such as; the sun, the stars, the Milky Way, the trees, the birds, the soil…etc. The way we view all things in our reality is a far and distant reality from truth. Instead, we can view these realities as beautiful pieces that make up the game and whenever one of these pieces in the puzzle no longer serves the game, we can feel comfortable enough to change it, or better yet, simply change our perception of it.

Chapter 3

Living in the Maya

We are currently living in a time of complete parallel opposites. Much of the world is totally lost in the illusion while on the other spectrum; there is a group of people on the planet that are waking up and a remembering unity consciousness (that is you!). I believe the best way to see where we currently sit in our consciousness is to look around us and notice what is happening. It is usually our direct environment that tells us where we are in our consciousness and what we are creating. When we turn our attention to a global viewpoint, we can see how all of our individual levels of consciousness are adding up to create the larger picture and story. Mahatma Gandhi always said "Be the change, you wish to see in the world." I love this quote because it is the truth. Every small part adds up to make the larger part. So as we change our internal environment to create more harmony, we contribute this back to the total experience upon Earth.

As I look to the Western world, I see a few ingredients that stand out to me. However, it may be different to you and your viewpoint so please try this exercise yourself. When I look at the Western World from the stand point of North America, I see a combination of the dependency on prescription medicines and obesity problems. I see the best selling books as motivation and self-improvement. I see a wide spread of yoga studios and alternative health care becoming more popular. If we traced our consciousness back 50 years ago, the acceptance of yoga and alternative therapies such as chiropractic surgery or energy healing was unheard of. Also obesity and the dependence of prescription drugs were not at its peak. As you can see, when one element moves up the ladder, its reflective counterpart mirrors its action.

I believe the reason for this is due to the old Chinese teachings of Ying and Yang. There is no dark without the light and vice versa. Collectively we are experiencing an interesting time in history from which all the ancient texts have pointed to, a shift occurring on the planet. We have traveled through time and become so lost in the illusion that humanity has forgotten their true identity. Many of the ancient texts call this the Maya.

The level of forgetfulness has become so extreme that projections and perceived separation on Earth between its people are at the highest ever to be seen. We find ourselves playing out a reality that does not completely serve our highest potential. We have become lost in the dream and thus forgetting that divine spark of wisdom inside.

For example, let's follow the story of a typical Joe Bloggs, who found himself lost in the dream.

Joe Bloggs, a 34 year old guy, lives an average life working at the bank. Growing up he always wanted to perform in the circus, yet since his dream was too abstract for his family to comprehend, he was put down for his dream and was shown another way to live. His parents put a lot of pressure on him to get good grades in school and if he did not get straight A's, then he would be punished and told he couldn't leave the house for a month, until his grades were back on track. This type of strict upbringing meant that by the age of 12, his dream to be a trapeze artist at the circus had surely disappeared and all he had time to focus on was his two toughest subjects math and arithmetic. Joe became quite depressed as a young child but continued to follow his parent's strict orders. Due to his depression, Joe would often find himself binging on candy and ice-cream in between study sessions. He developed a weight problem, which meant his once excited and fit body was no longer pulling him to run outside and do flips on the monkey bars, dreaming of the days in the circus. Joe's whole routine changed to staying indoors, studying, and watching moves on the weekends. As the years progressed, Joe was able to please his parents with a top job in a local financing firm, where he made a great wage, yet his belly was getting larger by the year and his habits of self criticism and guilt only grew stronger. By the time Joe was 34, he had no idea that he even had a problem. He considered his health to be normal in comparison to the people he spent time with and although he still found himself binging on the occasional donut and sabotaging himself with words of guilt, fear, and self blame, he considered himself to be normal.

Many people go through life believing that they are normal. Normal compared to whom? There is no such thing as normal. The only thing that makes an individual feel normal is if they can relate to the people that they are directly in contact with. The catch to this situation is that we tend to attract people into our life whom we do relate to. That makes us feel comfortable. However, if Joe decided to move to Africa, he would find that his perception of normal is far different than those living in such a place. Yet, the people living in Africa are also normal in comparison to the people they spend time with and I'm sure would perceive Joe to be strange or different.

What I propose is that instead of being comfortable with normal, how about stepping out of the box and following your inner guidance and live the life you have always dreamed of? When an individual decides to live the life they truly dream of, then often there will be people along the way that will tell you that they are silly or that it is unachievable. But the truth is, the only reason they are saying that is because they don't believe themselves personally could do it. And that's probably right. They couldn't do it because it's not their dream! The beautiful gift about having your own personal dream is that there is something so unique to that dream that only you can do. It is what you are coded with and it is born out of your inspiration.

If you asked a successful person "What is it that got you there?" I believe one of their answers would be the commitment to their inspiration. When a person feels inspired, the energy is unlimited because they are feeding from their life force. Inspired means in-spirit and the spirit is the life force energy that moves everything. The spirit or life force is eternal in it connects us to an eternal energy source. You could say that it is part of our pure consciousness, the oneness. Pure energy can never be destroyed, it can only change form, for example; you can start with an ice cube and then as the ice cube melts, the energy transforms into another state. Part of its physical expression turns into water, while the other parts goes through the process condensation and turns into vapor. The truth is the energy was not destroyed; just the image of what the ice cube now looks like.

So when we tap into spirit through our inspiration, we are able to transform ourselves into anything. Combining this power with the wisdom of tapping into our oneness and pure consciousness, you can almost guarantee that what we are transforming into is far more powerful than anything anyone could ever tell us is 'wrong'. When we are truly in this place of power, nothing that anyone could say or do would change our state of consciousness and our commitment to our truth. You can almost guarantee that people will try every role in the book to change your mind. They may put the guilt trip on you, blame, tears, anger, and try to pull at any strings, which have made you surrender in the past. These are all tests to see how much you can commit to your truth. The rewards from committing to your truth are infinitely more rewarding that the comforts you feel from making someone satisfied with their control. Sure, you may feel good for a while because it might make your relationship with that person 'better' and connected again, but sure enough, if you did not listen to your intuition the first time, then it will come knocking on your door and you will be presented with the same challenge again.

If you turn away your vision enough times, you will start to reprogram yourself to believe that you did not want the vision in the first place. This is when habits such as Joes overeating or binging on donuts comes into play. Every morning, Joe will make his way to the coffee and donut stand, putting on an additional few pounds each year. He would love to drop those extra kilos, yet there does not seem to be the inspiration to do so. Can anyone guess why?

When you are fully living the life of your dreams, inspiration then overflows into every part of your life. The reason being; when you feel good inside, you want to continue to do the things that make you feel good. These things may include; eating the right foods, exercising, thinking positive, lifting other people up to their life's vision, keeping a beautiful home, looking after your hygiene, nourishing your creativity, celebrating with good friends, and sharing in a balanced and inspired relationship.

If there is any area in your life that feels out of balance such as trouble with your relationships, a job you do not enjoy, financial difficulty, or health problems, then you can almost guarantee that there is something out of balance within your connection to yourself. You are not allowing yourself to be aware of the block or belief that is creating your difficulty. As mentioned in the previous chapter, the only way to true empowerment is through self-awareness. If you are not allowing yourself to be aware of those blocks, then your life will continue to be out of balance until you decide to do something about it.

For a moment, let us move ourselves back to Joe Bloggs, who is now working at the bank, a little over weight, unhappy and dissatisfied with his career, bored and judgmental of himself and others. His weight is a reflection of his self-esteem, which in many aspects connects back to him not living the life of his dreams. Since he started pushing his dream away at a very young age, Joe is not even aware as to why he is unhappy and overweight. Yet, Joe continues to plow away making a good wage but feeling more and more dissatisfied with his life, until one day he has a heart attack. The cholesterol from his poor eating habits has built up within the main arteries leading to his heart and finds it hard to pump anymore. Fortunately for him, he is raced to the hospital for surgery and they are able to dilate his blood so that it can move through efficiently once more. This frightens Joe as he had never thought at his age he would be faced with a near death experience. When the body reacts in such ways, the signposts are obviously screaming out for your attention. If Joe doesn't take this near death experience as a sign, then he will continue along the same path to no doubt, an early death. Perhaps his wise body may send him more signs, more heart attacks, but until he reads the signpost and learns the language of what his body is trying to tell him, he may never recover.

Fortunately, many people go through similar circumstances and wake up into realizing how precious and beautiful life is. Many others never wake up. A person's ability to wake up is dependent on how willing they are to become aware of their roadblocks. Sometimes looking at your road blocks can be too painful for a person to confront because it will mean a whole paradigm shift, which in affect would change everything from the relationships they share in their life, to the jobs they do. It will even change the habits they have and the way they seem themselves. Sometimes such a paradigm shift can be too frightening for someone. They prefer to live in the fear and doubt that created the roadblocks in the first place.

Don't feel bad if you are now thinking to yourself "Wow, I have some road blocks, but I don't know what they are." I would say 99% of the world's population is carrying around roadblocks: Some people more than others. It is the general state of where our world is that that creates these roadblocks. You are not to blame and neither are your parents, but rather it is a general flow that has occurred throughout history that has created our conditioning.

The world of illusion

As mentioned in Chapter 1, the world we live in today and the reality we create has often been lost in the continual projections of the mind. If we were to look at our planet's history, we would see a long trail of beliefs. Hierarchies and kingdoms rise and fall. When a new system such as a religion, a way of life, a tradition, or simply an opinion is born into the belief pattern of its people, life can drastically be changed for the good or for the bad. Ultimately, all systems of belief that are not connected to unity consciousness will eventually rise and fall. Some may last for centuries and others a few days. The element that allows a belief system to stay in reality is the consensus of those who believe it to be true. If there is a large enough group of people who believe the system of thought, then it will most likely stay around until someone challenges it and then the consensus changes.

You can see this take place in all the great Empires that ever lived. Adolf Hitler was a great example in the earlier part of our century. He had the power to shift millions of people to believe his propaganda, thus killing and mutilating thousands of people. The one ingredient that has the ability to change your consciousness and the world around you is certainty. Adolf Hitler was so certain of himself and his ideas about a pure race that he was able to influence and change the minds of all the people around him. It was his certainty that made people believe in him – that transformed his nation. This did not make his certainty correct, yet it was a great illusion that created a lot of unnecessary deaths.

Certainty in the world of illusion

Since we can now understand that everything that occurs in our world is a part of the illusion, we can have a good giggle at ourselves. This is the first step is recognizing the illusion. Once you have done that, you can forgive everyone else for the illusions they are creating. Although, just because you are able to recognize that you, along with many others, are living in illusion, does not mean that you have to put yourself into their game, because quite honestly not all games are fun. People will try to hold the greatest amount of certainty in their illusion to convince you to cross sides into their nightmare. So be aware when others are playing a seductive game of certainty.

Layers upon layers

For this part of the text, let's look at the individual person whom you see shopping at the local market. Often times we are so caught in our illusion that we do not notice all the illusions and baggage people are carrying around. As you turn your attention inwardly to being aware of yourself, you are able to become aware of those people around you. Part of self-mastery is being able to peel off your layers while the other half comes when you assist others in peeling of theirs as well. So next time you go into the local grocery market, turn your attention to being aware of those around you. I'm not asking you to approach anyone, just observe. Notice how they are walking. Do they have a straight back or are they hunched over? Do they move toward their direction with their nose or their hips, or what part of their body moves them forward? What is the pigmentation of their skin? What body language do they express? Try not to stare at people. I know it may be a little tricky, but the best way to make this exercise flow is by being inconspicuous. As you start to notice all these elements of a person, you will start to see what type of thought projection they are carrying around. This is the belief of who they think they are their identity. This type of exercise will assist you in becoming more in tune with those people around you. When you are in tune with people around you, you can assist them because you become more compassionate in holding space for them to grow rather than reacting to their beliefs or what thoughts they are throwing at you. When we are able to truly see the person and the programs they carry around, we are able to step into a whole new level of awareness in that relationship. Often we find our selves cursing our neighbor, or gossiping about their habits because we feel offended by them. Yet the only element that feels offended is our ego. Our ego is the illusion that also resonates with that problem. To step out of the illusion is to become aware of it. So next time you decide to gossip about someone or you feel let down by someone's actions, instead of pointing fingers, decide to look deeper and see where their actions came from. You might find something quite surprising that makes you reach out in compassion rather than offence.

One thing that I've noticed is that the more someone is lost in the illusion, the more they try to recreate themselves in the physical dimension. You can see this through continual and obsessive shopping. The styles of clothes, identities people adopt, and the things people say all serve as examples. This can become quite a problem in most circles of people as individuals are walking around with their labels, what job they do, what their name is, their status in life, who their parents are, what country or town they came from…etc. All of these systems of thought can contribute to a person's identity crisis because the moment any of these elements are threatened, their life and their identity is also threatened. That means they have to go find another identity somewhere else. What happens when someone's identity is threatened?

The moment a child is born, they are given their identity. They learn from the people around them who they are and what is right and wrong. All of these beliefs given to the child will then shape the child's personality and how they perceive life. The moment those beliefs are tested, watch out! Let's take our attention now to an area in the world where the dream many people are living is a nightmare. Let's take a look in Uganda, Africa, where children were once and many still are being trained as boy soldiers, kidnapped away from their families at a very young age and brainwashed to be killing machines and their master being the head of the rebels. Those children have been through some of the most severe types of conditioning to an extent where some of them even sneak back to their town where they will rape and pillage their own family. Many children have been rescued from this hard life and are on their way to waking up again. Others are still trapped in the walls of their mental conditioning and confusion, continually projecting their programmed thoughts into reality. In a life such as this, everything is at stake. The food they eat, where they sleep, and the life they live. To live in this dream would surely be a nightmare since allowing yourself a moment of peace would be very hard, as you never know who's holding a gun to your head.

Forgetting ourselves in the Maya

All of these pressures of trying to hold your identity can make us forget the truth of who we are and where we come from – which is the pure consciousness unified by all things. When a person's identity starts to fall, this is perhaps the most frightening time in anyone's life. That's why some people find it hard to die while others are more graceful with their departure. For someone who is conditioned to believe that they are their body, then that body dying would be the hardest thing to let go of. This works in the same way for someone who identifies themselves through their beauty and glamour. The moment their heal breaks on their stiletto shoes is a moment of complete embarrassment, or the boxer who identifies himself as the best boxer in the nation and then gets beat by his competitor. All of these examples show you how when someone's identity is threatened, embarrassment, fear, or even strong waves of emotional pain appear. If the person is completely attached to that identity, then other areas of their life will begin to be hampered by the collapse of the other. For example, if someone is identified by their partner in life and they lose their partner either through a death or simply a bad break up, then the individual completely identified by the relationship may suffer an array of problems which will then affect the rest of their life.

Here is a story of Jane and Larry who found themselves in a relationship for over 5 years. Jane is head over heels in love with

Larry since he has provided for her and offered safety and comfort from her fears in life. He has financially supported her and emotionally comforted her when she needed a shoulder to cry on. Larry on the other hand, was somewhat more comfortable and after 5 years found that his girlfriend was becoming far too needy and demanding of his time. He was no longer able to hang out with his friends or do the things he used to be so fond of. Jane was so wrapped up in Larry that she believed she had found her soul mate. However, he must do everything that she demanded or she was not happy. After five years, Larry finally finds the courage to let Jane know that he is no longer interested in maintaining a relationship with her. In response, Jane is devastated. Her whole identity now feels threatened. Who will provide for her? Support her emotionally and fill the void in her heart? Since Jane has never developed self-awareness, Jane is forced into a painful illusion based on fear and separation. This could then lead Jane into further acts of self-destruction such as depressive eating, loss of motivation at work, negative thinking, and a whole array of patterns of self-destruction. On the other hand, Larry may feel self-empowered. For the first time, he stood up for himself and demanded a life he wanted to live. This may give Larry more motivation to be the person he has always dreamed of.

After many weeks of self-sabotage, doubt and fear, Jane finally realizes that in order to be happy, she must get over Larry and find her own happiness. This leaves her an option. Does she decide to find a partner who can once again fulfill her void or does she start to practice self-awareness and remember who she is again? If Jane were able to get in touch with her pain in a way that teaches her self-awareness, she would understand where her fears came from. In understanding her fears, she would be able to move into a greater place of loving herself. When a person allows himself or herself to move into those uncomfortable feelings created in the illusion, they're able to see where their issues first came from. But if you never allow yourself the time to look, then you will continue to project the same patterns into your life, repeating the same stories. The beautiful element to allowing yourself to reflect and become aware is that in doing so, you start to feel change occurring and a greater intelligence working for you.

Agreements in the Maya

As a human being, we are always making agreements while living in the illusion. Some of the agreements are aligned to the benefit of your highest truth while other agreements are made through yours or another person's agenda to fulfill the void in their awareness. When a person is not completely aware of their unity with all things, agendas are born and are usually played on the subtle field. They may be invisible to the physical eye, yet the power they hold on individuals can be potent. It is important to reflect upon our intentions in all situations and be clear about our true intentions as we evolve in our ability to know ourselves. Otherwise we begin playing in a field of the illusionist, saying one thing but doing another.

In our semi-aware state, many of us are not even aware of the agendas other people are playing in our life because they are so subtle. It is only when we truly know ourselves that we can spot this kind of player a mile away. One way to tune yourself into this awareness is to simply ask how a person makes you feel when they present you with a proposition. Does it make you feel inspired from the very core of your soul or do you feel a question within your psyche that you can't quite put your finger on? This feeling of an unknown question is usually your natural intelligence decoding what's happening on the subtle field. It is your intelligence that feels there is more to this request than meets the eye. The bottom line is that if anyone requests that you do something that you are not completely comfortable with, do not do it! Maybe they try pulling on the guilt strings, or using reverse psychology or another type of peer pressure? Whatever the tactic, be aware if you don't feel completely comfortable, then this is a message from your soul telling you that there is another agenda at play.

For example, imagine that you are out hunting for a car and you head into the local dealership where you see a car that strikes your interest. Upon taking the car for a test drive, the salesman says to you "I have another person interested in buying this, so if

you do not put it on hold today, it might not be here tomorrow".
You look at the salesman and something doesn't feel right. In this
case, let's presume that what the car salesman says is not
completely accurate. There may be another person interested, but
the salesman knows the car will most likely still be there
tomorrow. In this case, he's projecting an idea into your
consciousness to make you feel fear so that you will get the car
today! As you look at the salesman, you feel uncomfortable and
you believe the reason is because you do not want to lose the car.
But in fact, this feeling is coming from his ulterior motive. Since
you are a trusting person, you tell yourself that it must be your fear
that's making you uncomfortable.

If there is any dynamic in your life that is bringing up fear,
you should ask yourself "where is it coming from?" If it is coming
from an outside pressure then you will know that there is an
agenda at play. However if it is coming from an inside pressure
(from yourself) this is a great opportunity for growth.

Outside Pressure vs. Inside Pressure

Outside pressure is when someone places an intense energy on
you out of his or her personal expectations and motives. When this
intense energy makes you feel uncomfortable or obliged, then you
know it's their own agenda that they are trying to intertwine you in.
On the other hand, inside pressure is your soul pushing you for
personal growth. This inside pressure usually feels a lot different
than an outside pressure because it resides from the core of your
being and its only intention is for you to grow into a greater you.
Let us use an example of inside pressure versus outside pressure.

Assume that you are dating a new man/women in your life and
whenever you spend time with them, you feel yourself growing in
leaps and bounds and time feels effortless when you are together.
You feel inspired to be around them. But when you are apart, your
friends feel jealous and try every move in the book to keep your
attention with them since they fear loosing their best friend. Of
course, your friends do not tell you that they are jealous. Due to
their insecurity of not knowing their true unity to all things, they
start projecting an unconscious agenda to have you all to

themselves. Maybe they use the guilt trip when you want to hang out with your new lover by telling you that you are being disrespectful of them or that you have already made commitments to them. Maybe they feed you small little white lies that may divert your attention from sharing time with the person you truly want. All of these actions are placed into the field and are part of your friends' agenda to keep you close. But on the surface, they do not present it that way. This is an example of outside pressure. Now you feel conflicted with what you truly want and the pressure from an outside source is having you do what they want (which is to fulfill their ego's fear).

The inside pressure brings up feelings of inspiration to move forward upon certain tasks. Sometimes inside pressure can also bring up fears, yet there is an undercurrent that tells you that by tackling this fear you are going to feel amazing. The fear from an inside pressure (created by yourself) is usually related to a perceptional roadblock which you picked up somewhere. For example, there may be someone at work you have wanted to ask out for months now, as you feel inspired whenever you are around them. At the same time, you fear rejection if you ask them out. This fear of rejection is the roadblock, created in your mind. It was probably created the last time you were rejected in a relationship or through a related experience. However, there is an internal pressure that keeps coming up within you to ask him/her out and it will keep pushing you until you get over the road block. As you move through these roadblocks, your internal environment starts to feel more expansive and free because you are following your internal guidance and acting upon your internal pressure.

If you keep responding to outside pressure when it doesn't match your inside pressure, then you'll forever feel unfulfilled. Maybe you will feel good for a short while because you made someone happy? But unless you are following your own happiness scale then this happiness will always be dependent upon other people and will be short lived. To make matters worse, the problem will not go away. If you are continually responding to outside pressure and not honoring your inner pressure then more and more outside pressures will build up until you finally reach a point of breakdown where you either get sick, or feel emotionally or mentally exhausted because you keep trying to make other people happy rather than making yourself happy.

It's nice to do things for other people, but unless it is in tune with your true inner happiness, then it will continue to feel like a burden and sooner or later, you will get exhausted.

Here are a few questions to see if you're reacting to outside pressure:

- Do you do things for other people because you feel guilty?
- Do you fear how people will react when you follow your heart?
- Are you tiptoeing around others because of their insecurities?
- Do you make decisions based on peer pressure?
- Do you sometimes compromise your morals to get what you want?
- Are you ever confused with what your heart truly wants?

If you answered yes to any of the above questions, then you are compromising your true happiness for the agendas of those around you. Remember that most of the time; those around you may not even know they are operating on an agenda. That is because the fears that create their agendas are so unconscious and deep. It is usually not necessary to approach these people about their agendas unless you believe that they may be open to looking at them. All that is really necessary is that you become aware of these agendas and start responding; not to the outside pressure, but the inside pressure.

Here are a few questions to see if you are responding to inside pressure:

- Are you aware of what your heart truly wants?
- Do you act upon the beautiful feelings in your heart?
- Do you nourish the experiences that bring you inspiration?
- Do you feel strong in communicating and living from your hearts pure intentions?
- Do you place your inner happiness and connection above all things?
- Do you follow your intuitive impulses, regardless of the opinions of others?

If you answered yes to any of these questions, then you are moving into a place of acting upon your true inner guidance based on your inner pressure. We must always remember that anything that comes from our intuition is of a much higher order than anyone's agenda could ever be. By acting on your intuitive guidance, others may not always be happy because it could mean that there outside pressure has no result on your life and they may not get what they want. This can frustrate others when they realize they have no control over you. However, it's a great aid for them since it will move them into reflecting upon their own insecurities in order to heal their patterns of disconnection. Upon living through your heart and your intuitive guidance, you are still able to be open and loving to those around you. It doesn't take away your ability to love them. In reality, it gives you more ground to assist them in looking at their own blocks and programs and I would say this is greatest love you could show anyone.

When Outside Pressure meets Inside Pressure

The best type of outside pressure comes when it matches your inside pressure. This is when the desires of those around you match the desires you also wish for. For example, after many years of eating fast food, you decide it is time to get into shape. So you join the gym. While at the gym, you bring on a personal trainer who can teach you a run of exercises while pushing you to be your best. Every day that you share a session with your instructor, you feel him pushing you just a little further. It's tough and you are sweating like never before and on top of that, the trainer keeps pushing you to do one more lift. You could give up, yet you know that this outside pressure connects to your inside pressure. Visions of a brand new body, unbeatable health, and abundant energy run through your mind. So you keep lifting and although it's uncomfortable, you feel gratitude for the outside pressure as it makes your internal relationship stronger.

Are you playing a game of agenda?

Since we are now capable of seeing if someone else is imposing their agenda upon our life, I think it would be wise to see if we are placing any agendas on those around us. Let's remember that agendas usually come from a place within ourselves where we feel a disconnection from unity. While in this place of disconnection, fears usually pop up in the weirdest places. So do not be hard on yourself if you realize that you have also been operating on agendas. Agendas are only harmful if they are played in the subtle unconscious field. So if you find out that you have been operating through an agenda, all you have to do is come clean with your intentions. Often people are scared to be completely honest with their intentions because they fear the other person will say no. In response, they create these unconscious agendas, which are implemented with very little discussion, yet often at times a great deal of pressure.

Here are some questions to ponder:

- Do you ever say one thing, but mean something totally different?
- Have you ever used guilt on someone to get what you want?
- Do you ever use anger to make someone do something?
- Have you ever put someone down to make yourself feel better?
- Have you ever forced your opinion upon someone, even when they didn't ask for it?
- Have you ever taken something from someone without asking?

If you have answered yes to any of these questions, then yes, like most of us, you have played a game of agenda. These agendas can be the cruelest game because without realizing it, you are attempting to control someone through their weakness. If you have ever been susceptible to someone else's agenda, then you know exactly how it feels and you are probably making a commitment right now to not to be controlled by other peoples insecurities. While making that decision, let's make a decision to be more aware of our own insecurities and ourselves. If we are able to keep a diary beside our bed and write down our feelings every night, we might start to get a greater knowledge of what is truly happening in the unconscious mind. When we are able to watch our insecurities,

44

they have less control over us. Life can be a lot easier when we are aware of what we truly desire. That's because instead of going around the bush and creating agendas to get what we want, we are able to go directly to the person and communicate our intention clearly. If the answer is no, you can move on. This makes life a lot simpler and clearer.

Fear of "No"

There is an ingrained fear within all of humanity and that is the word "NO". Why? From the moment we are born, denial of anything has been labeled as bad. It is a word that offends the ego and creates embarrassment, anger, fear, and doubt in a person. Let's have a look at the word no and why everyone is so petrified of it.

As we bring ourselves down to the most basic needs, we can see that food and water are of the simplest necessity. As a newborn child enters the world, they too come through with these basic needs, yet they have no way of communicating them. If we were all as highly intuitive as we potentially could be, then we would be more in tune with our child and hear the thought waves coming from our beloved newborn as they ask for fresh milk. However, since we are not equipped enough with these full intuitive abilities, this child may be asking for hours and the only response it is getting is a big fat "NO!" Until it becomes so fed up that it starts to scream and creates a tantrum to express an onslaught of emotions that get mom's attention. The no factor has put so much fear in the child, that in order to get any response it must scream, cry, and change its whole body chemistry of harmony in order to get someone's attention and get the nourishment it desires.

As the child grows up, it has now realized that shifting its body chemistry to tears is a great way to get what they want, even though this is potentially unhealthy. The beautiful element to this part of the process is that the child is so clear and honest about its agenda that it's not hiding a thing at all. Later on in life, the child may realize that simply screaming and asking for food is not the best way to get food. Instead they could steal and cheat or better yet, get a job and buy their own food.

The way a human being behaves has a lot to do with its upbringing and how well received the child's intentions are, as well as the care given to the child when answered no. If the child receives a no, yet does not understand the wisdom behind it, then you can guarantee that there's now one more layer of fear added to the child surrounding the word no. But if you can share an understanding as to why your answer is no, then the fear around this simple word would be lessened.

If the child is taught to fear the word no, then this hidden agendas come into play. The person becomes so fearful that they will not get what they want (since their whole life was a big fat no) that they will now use other tactics to get it.

The following are some questions that will help you to look at potential agenda patterns.

- Do you fear asking directly for your desires: such as in relationships, finance, work, and family?
- Do you fear being let down?
- Have you ever stopped following your dream because someone told you no?
- Are you afraid of the word no?
- Are their certain topics that you feel awkward discussing?

If you answered yes to any of these questions then there may be some potential roadblocks that are affecting your life today. As mentioned earlier, these roadblocks usually come from an immature space of not understanding the wisdom behind no. Now that we are adults, we are able to look 'no' square in the face and ask "why?"

When we are able to ask why, then we are able to comprehend the wisdom behind it. One we have found the wisdom, we can reshape and put actions to make it a yes, or perhaps we may even realize that no was the best answer after all. For example, maybe you are trying out for the state basketball team and you really want to get in. So at the last minute you start training with only a few months until try-outs. Yet you are so keen to get in that you work extra hard. By the time try-outs come along, you come so close yet are not selected. Off go the sirens screaming at you "NO!" This "no" could make you doubt your performance and if you are really hurt by the decline, you may wish to stop basketball all together.

However, if you had allowed yourself to look further into the "no" you may realize that you were closer than you thought and just a little bit more training and attention to your shooting skills, you could be in by next year. As you can see, by looking further into the "no" wisdom can be found and the pain, anger, or potential sorrow that many feel will disappear a lot quicker than if you held onto the "no" and never asked the question.

So next time you have a desire to create something in your life, recognize that asking for it directly is not a bad thing. Perhaps you may get a "no" but even the "no" is going to give you more wisdom for growth. So don't be afraid of your dreams and expressing them!

Chapter 4

Contraction & Expansion

The Swinging Pendulum

We live in a field of continual balance and the way I choose to look at reality is like a pendulum that swings. If the pendulum swings back drastically, it is obviously going to swing forward in the same pace until after a while the swings are not so high and low and the velocity and speed slowly decrease. This is the process of all things. That is why it's important to remember that although there may seem to be large amounts of perceived bad, there is also equal good which plays the other role in the swinging pendulum idea. So we could say that no matter how much terror and horror there is, there will always be just as much "good" to balance it out. You may not always see the good but on a collective and individual level, energies are always balancing. As this world goes through the darkest times, we can see the brightest times coming in to balance it. For every threatening disease, you can bet there will soon be a solution. For every wrong, there will soon be a right. In human consciousness, this comes from a place not of wanting to do well, but out of the survival of our species. For example, with all the fuss and fear of global warming, we are now seeing some of the greatest technologies come out to create sustainable solutions. Some examples include electric cars or the wide spread of solar heating and wind technologies – the list goes on. I can bet that if the world were not faced with the current challenges of global warming, the balancing of all these new technologies would not be streaming through. Why? Because people would not be as motivated. Therefore, governments might not provide as much money for solutions and individuals would not be as interested in creating solutions. As you can see, with every challenge we face there is always a counter energy to match it in equal proportion. It just so happens that the time that we live in is forcing the pendulum to swing at almighty highs and lows. Therefore we're getting tossed around like a boat in a high tide storm. The waves are throwing us around and all we can do is grab onto the side of the ship and hope the waves will soon settle.

So what happens when the waves do settle, or in the case of the pendulum, the swings become less intense? This is a time when all the challenges are being solved and as each challenge is solved the swing looses its velocity, ultimately balancing life back into a more peaceful flow that results in a less intense reality. Just picture the swinging pendulum as it slows itself down; every moment becomes gentler and less intense. By becoming aware of this one fact you can now ask yourself the following questions. What part of this scenario am I playing in? Am I adding to the devastating lows of mine and our collective Earth's reality or am I providing solutions to balance out the lows, thus bringing myself and the world back into equilibrium?

Here are a few questions that may assist you in seeing whether or not you are contributing to the lows:

- Am I involved in a job that doesn't serve life, such as people, animals, and environment?
- Am I the type of person who likes to create drama in my life?
- Do I leave the lights on even when I'm not in the room?
- Am I the type of person to gossip about others?
- Do I support a group that's against other religions or races?

The truth is most of us are a part of the lows as much as the highs. Here are some questions to see if you are contributing in any way to the high swings.

- Do I purchase environmentally clean products instead of toxic products?
- Do I contribute my time or money to any worthy causes that supports life? Some examples would be a non-profit organization, animal shelter, or environmental cause.
- Do I lift people up and make them feel good about themselves?
- Do I always remember to turn the lights off when I leave a room?

• Am I inclusive of everyone around me by honoring and respecting their beliefs, regardless of my own opinion?

These are just a few questions to see how you can be a part of our planet's collective growth. Ultimately it is all working to balance each other out and the more focus we put into creating solutions, the less the problems will overtake the world. That means that we don't have to over exhaust our energy to return it to balance. So by choosing to do some good every day, we will slowly make our way back to our center.

When we are in our center (whether that be as a planet or simply as individuals) we're able to live a life, which is far more effortless. When I say center what I mean is no drama and complete health in all aspects. For example an individual who is off center in their life could be really sick and is continually in and out of hospital. This person, no matter what illness it may be, would continually feel out of center. Maybe their brain feels foggy from all the drugs they have been fed or the state of their pain affects their ability to walk, talk, or even breath. This is an image of someone who is not in his or her center. Life to them has become a huge effort; therefore in order to do anything they must exert a large amount of energy to complete a task as simple as breathing.

Now let's look at someone who is in the center and paint a picture of them – someone who exercises every day, finds time to still their mind, eats the right foods, and admires beauty in all things. This person has found balance in body, mind, and spirit. All other endeavors seem to happen with very little effort. It's systematic and doesn't need any thought to orchestrate. The person is simply living in their natural state and no effort is required.

If we were to compare this same equation to the current state of the world, we would see the same results. Right now, there is a lot of problems – from disease within the human race, pollution of our environment, our lack of connection to our wider family on the planet called wildlife, and a general pollution of the air. As you can see, there are many areas, which are out of balance. As mentioned before, whatever swings in one direction will certainly swing in the other direction. So in response, we as a species are now faced with a greater challenge to change the course of our individual, as well as our planet's future. More effort is now required to make the changes, in the same way a sick person must focus on his healing in order to survive. As our planet returns to full health, we will notice that the whole system of how our planet operates would have changed and we will be more in tune with the harmony of nature around us. This will mean less dependency on technologies that kill our environment and ourselves and rather focusing on elements that sustain life and lift us into a greater state of being. When we reach this place, life will once again be a lot more effortless and just like the person who lives a healthy life with good exercise, diet, and positive thinking, the flow of our planet will be based on a greater intelligence and once again flow effortlessly.

We are consciousness

Whenever there is an energy that is out of balance, you can guarantee that there is an unconscious block to the unity of all elements of life, which includes the love and respect for your body, your thoughts, your environment and the people around you, the animals, and every vibrating particle of life. As we develop our ability to be completely conscious and present, our reverence for life expands. Initially, the reverence that you hold may just be for yourself. Then perhaps you may expand your reverence to your dog and your family, and then your local community, your country, the world, the animals and then hopefully all of it inhabitants regardless of their system of belief, culture, status or way of life. When we are able to move into greater awareness of our unity to all things, our heart opens up in to a greater understanding for all life. There is no limit to the reverence and love you can hold because it's forever expanding and only becomes more fulfilling the more you tap into it.

For example, let's start off with someone who has very little awareness of his or her interconnectedness to all things. Maybe this person found himself or herself lonely and living on the street. They defend their cardboard box every night and fight for the last serving of food at the local food drop off point. Some nights there is no food, other nights it is cold and they only have one blanket to wrap them up in warmth. This person through their level of consciousness lives their life based on survival and due to this fact, they have decided to alienate everyone around them in order to fend for themselves. They don't have a supportive partner in their life, nor do they have much energy to do anything other than sleep and put their hand out for a small token of food. This type of case is usually combined with not only a poor diet, but also sometimes an escape from reality that may be through drugs or alcohol. This propels their body into further discomfort and disconnection from the effortless flow.

Opening up

If this person was able to open up by becoming aware of some potentially dangerous habits, they may be able to create a greater level of unity to their direct environment. What if the person who sleeps in the cardboard hut next to him tapped on their wall one cold evening, and said, "Would you mind snuggling with me, I'm cold?" And what if this person replied, "Yes" and they developed a friendship through supporting each other. Both of these people have now opened themselves to a greater unity in their direct environment by welcoming in a new energy. And, since we are talking about welcoming new energies in, what if these two people then decided to motivate each other by creating a small business and they start washing windows of cars at the traffic lights? This one action of working together would propel them into greater levels of expansion, creating additional feelings of unity with the greater world around them. They would then be connecting with more people and feeling better about themselves and their reality. Every time someone takes a step into greater unity, they feel better within themselves and their environment. That propels them forward, picking up speed as it travels. One good deed leads to another good deed and so forth.

You can tell a lot about where your consciousness is by reflecting on your direct environment. As I discussed earlier, symbols are found in your direct environment and situation is the grandest example of your state of consciousness. This doesn't mean that you have to be living in a five-story palace to be connected to unity. Actually, many people living in a five-story palace carry similar frequencies of consciousness to those living in a cardboard box on the street. The similarity is that the person living in big house may still be all alone and fearful of leaving the protection of their gated community - fearful of other people and life's challenges. This is a lot like the person in the cardboard hut. The difference between the two is the belief about themselves. The greater belief and more self esteem you have within yourself, the more you can create the life you truly dream of. Perhaps the person living in the 5-story mansion was brought up in a very wealthy family. Money was never a struggle for them. Therefore, they carry a belief around with them that money comes naturally and this belief and vibration puts them in alignment with creating this reality. However, the other person may have been raised on the streets and learned to fight for money and survival. As you can see, these two belief systems would make you behave a lot differently.

All states of consciousness if disconnected from unity will result in dissatisfaction. The reason being is that there will be a feeling that there needs to be something else to complete you. A feeling of emptiness and loneliness will be the under current of your reality. This is why I say that it doesn't matter what your circumstances appear to be on the surface, it's the quality of your consciousness that paints your world. There are many people out there who are the biggest social butterflies. They have all the friends in the world but at the end of the day, they still come home feeling lonely. There are also a whole bunch of loners out there who are so connected to the unity in everything that they feel fulfilled and overflowing.

If we go back to the simple understanding that we are vibrating fields of energy connected to everything else, then we are able to tap into the fact that everything in our field is connected. As we strip away the labels on things, we can start to see that all energies contain information. This information has a certain energetic structure that makes it have a certain personality and quality. The more physical energy systems (like mater) are easier to read in terms of the information they hold on the physical plane. But what about if we started peeling back the physical plane and started reading the energy itself. We are all capable of doing this, yet we just don't realize it. Have you ever walked into a room and felt the tension between certain individuals? In these circumstances, no words or physical expressions are needed to sense it.

We have all been accustomed to read energies. Yet, since it is an element that cannot be seen with the human eye, many of us do not believe we can do it. As we become more aware of our individual energy system and peel of all the layers, we are able to have more certainty in the energy we read in others. Often times when we are not completely clear within our own energy system (such as carrying around unconscious programs) we may think we are being intuitive. But we are really just projecting our own insecurities onto others. Let's look at another example. Your boss may have moved you to a different department and you are so furious and believe he did it because he thought you were lazy. In this instance, you start bitching to your friend about how lazy and inconsiderate your boss is. This potential illusion (if incorrect) could propel you forward into more discomfort, rather than coming from the heart and deciding to talk to him about it.

The properties of expansion and contraction

When working through the illusion of life, we often go through stages of contraction and expansion. Contraction is usually related to the inward motion and the internal reflection, this space when out of balance can turn into victim mentality and send the body, mind and spirit into its ultimate space of ego and separation, causing illness and the breaking down of your physical body. Expansion is the energy that comes forth from knowing your true interconnectedness with all things – a state of knowing and trust. This propels you into a state of enthusiasm to move into life with effortless grace, expanding into new dimensions.

Think back to a time when you felt on top of the world. Maybe you had just fallen in love or received a promotion at work. Or perhaps you were just relaxing on a holiday vacation. There are an infinite amount of situations that can make a person feel this way. As we clear our conditioned mind, we start to see that we can feel this all day and every day, regardless of the circumstances. However, for this exercise let's recall a time when life was making you jump for joy! As you think back to this time, tune into your body and see how it feels. Notice the openness in your chest, the lightness in your body, and feel the energy running through your system? Also, what types of thoughts are circulating in your mind and how you perceive everything around you. This is a feeling of expansion. Normally in these states, you are a lot more aware of your environment, the people around you, and your connection to everything. These are the feelings that remind you that everything is unified. In this mode, the individual is usually very optimistic and supportive of the greater world around them.

Now think back to a time when you were having a really bad day. Maybe your boyfriend/girlfriend just dumped you? Or you were fired from work or your pet dog died? Zone into your body and see how your body feels. Maybe your shoulders are hunched over, you feel a twist in your stomach, you are short of breath from the tightness in your chest, or you feel heaviness. Notice the types of thoughts that are circulating your mind and how you perceive everything around you. These are all feelings of contraction and in this state, you are less aware of the environment around you – the people, the places, and your connection to all things. The reason for this is because when experiencing contraction you are collapsing your attention on the greater oneness. When completely out of balance, contraction mode can turn into self-pity and playing the victim, which can send the person down a spinning spiral.

Contraction can aid expansion at times as long as the contraction doesn't turn into victim mode. Contraction can be used to take time out, assess information, and even find wisdom in areas of confusion. Although a lot of the time, the mind likes to get involved in this process and ends up creating a whole bunch of stories based on the person's perception and roadblocks.

If a person is able to step into unity consciousness when they feel a challenge arise in their life, they are able to bypass the chatter of the projecting mind and step right into the wisdom of their true nature. In this state, they will find whatever it is they are looking for. Usually it surrounds letting go, forgiveness, and a realization of deep gratitude.

By moving into unity consciousness, the contraction of your experience is gently loved back into its true nature, which is expansiveness. The expansiveness is the part of us that knows its connection to the greater whole. When we are aware of this, we realize that anything is possible and that we are infinite beings.

Consciousness in the body temple

The whole body, physical, mental, emotional, and spiritual, is a vibrating energy field that holds different systems of information. The spiritual body is the finest vibration system to the whole being. It's the element that holds everything together and where everything is shaped. This part of the body is the lightest in frequency and is connected to all of the ethereal realms of consciousness and holds the truest and brightest expression of your potential. The mental body is the controller of all your thoughts that are fed through your system. This is the part of your body that filters information and decides what to believe and what not to believe. The emotional body is the next level down in density and holds various octaves of frequency, depending on the emotion. This emotion is created through the perception of your mental body and how it relates to your direct reality and your desires. Finally, the physical body is the densest in frequency. This part of your body creates the appearance of your image to those who see with physical eyes.

All levels of the body hold layers of information and when each layer is connected to unity consciousness, you have a perfect replica of a human body, mind, emotion, and spirit that is in balance on all levels and all systems. Since we currently live in a world that is breaking free from much of the destructive illusions, you can bet that there would not be a whole lot of people who are completely balanced in all levels of their energy system. As we continue to get in touch with unity consciousness, we are able to cleanse the walls of perception and heal any areas of our system that have come out of balance.

When someone is diagnosed with an "incurable" disease, they are being fed a reality based on a belief disconnected to unity. Since there's a lack of education in the consciousness within the greater world, most of these diagnoses become a reality. The person gives up on life the moment they are fed this illusion. But if a person were to connect to the greater version of themselves through self-awareness techniques, they would be able to move through each system of their body and become aware of what lives there. Any type of disease in the body is the physical manifestation of contracted information in the body.

Let's look at some of the key principles and information held in contraction when it out of balance:

- Loss of unity
- Caving in of energy
- Thoughts of self doubt, sabotage and victim
- Hatred towards one self and others
- An unconscious belief that you do not deserve to live

The following are key principles they come from a feeling of expansion:

- Feelings of unity with all people, places, and things in your environment
- Posture in alignment, heart open
- Thoughts of empowerment, potential, and enthusiasm
- Love toward yourself and others
- A knowingness of your connection to oneness

One amazing book that I'd recommend to anyone who is dealing with a disease in the body is Louise Hays, best seller: You Can Heal Your Life. This book goes into detail on the emotional causes for all problems in the physical body.

Wherever your disease has started is usually the best place in the body to first place your attention. There are countless techniques that you can use to get in touch with the information locked in your body. Once you are able to tap into the information that is causing the disease, you are able to move through it and heal it. Any type of disease in the body is just an area of your consciousness that has not received the attention and love that it deserves. Yet, you have the power to give it the attention and heal anything.

A lot of the time people become so frightened by the diagnosis of the doctor that they get structured into the reality of black and white. However, when we remember that there is a gray area that unifies the black and the white, we remember that there may be other alternatives and other ways of viewing the situation.

The thing about our current state of consciousness is that everyone is looking to label everything and give it a definition. If it doesn't hold a definition, then we are taught that it is to be feared. As we step away from defining certain elements in our life, we give ourselves permission to make mistakes and be more counter intuitive.

So now that you have decided to let go of the labels that define your disease, you are able to look at the real information. Not the information of what it is called, but rather the information of what you are truly storing in your body. Since everything is energy, it makes sense that we should be able to transform this energy out of our system.

Transforming energy blocks: Disease to health

The following are some ways to bring awareness back into your body. This can help when you're feeling healthy or when you are working through a physical, mental, or emotional disease. If you are working through some more intense levels of disease, then it might be a good idea to have a friend there who can just support you through your process, since it may bring up larger emotions.

1. Lay down in a comfortable zone and turn off all electronics including TV, radio, phones etc.
2. Cover yourself in something cozy and make sure you are in a place away from disturbances.
3. Close your eyes and feel the sensations throughout your body.
4. Notice any areas of discomfort. These are the areas where information has not been understood, therefore creating a block and physical discomfort
5. Place your hand on any area on your body where you feel discomfort
6. Feel the sensations in this area (this is the process of bringing awareness to the unconscious).
7. As you feel these sensations, ask your body what information it wishes to communicate to you.
8. Feel deeper into the sensations of the body (by placing this level of attention of the body, you are reminding yourself that you care deeply).

9. As information comes up surrounding the discomfort in your body, remind yourself to be gentle and forgiving of whatever information comes through.
10. When coming out of this meditation, write down any affirmations you can think of that allow you to balance out the previous programs in your body that you discovered.
11. Stick these affirmations up in places where you are most likely to see them often – such as in your car, your bathroom mirror, on your desk, or the fridge.

The information that you receive in these sessions may not have anything to do with the subtle body, but may have to do with a particular emotion, a thought, or belief about yourself or even a circumstance that occurred in your life earlier on. Whatever information comes up, simply honor the process, no matter how abstract it is. Remember that by placing your awareness on the body, you are waking up those areas that have become unconscious. In the process of waking up the unconscious, everything becomes conscious again, and when all is conscious there is a remembrance of your true unity with everything.

Transferring levels of consciousness

Have you ever noticed after spending time with some people you feel alive, motivated, and full of inspiration? And when spending time with others, you walk away feel depleted and exhausted? This is the transfer of consciousness from one person to another. As we walk through the great illusion of life, we are continually being bombarded with illusion after illusion. Sometimes the illusion is fun to play as it create a fun game and everyone is happy, while at other times the illusion creates horrible feelings of disconnection and lack of joy. Which game are you playing?

If you are the type of person who finds themselves continually dealing with drama, gossip, and swinging highs and lows, then I'd say that you are allowing the game to play you. That means you have very little control over the general balance of your reality. However, if you seem to be living a joyful life for the most part and continually have a smile on your face, then I would say you are mastering your game. You're the type of person people want to be around because you lift them up and remind them how magical and wonderful life is.

Since we are all vibrating fields of consciousness, we have an opportunity to create different realities wherever we go. By choosing to co-create with others around us, we bring a lot more enjoyment to the game. When we move into victim mode, we automatically stop the co-creation process with others and are left in a very lonely game.

As you spend time with other people, decide to be aware of the energy that's being transferred through your interaction. By placing awareness on this element, you are expanding your skill set and knowledge to how energy really works. Since we are energy and we now understand that all energy holds information, we can see that by spending time with another person, energy and information is going to be exchanged. This happens mostly on the unconscious level. When we interact with another, our attention is usually focused on a few ingredients such as the flow of the conversation, the environment, and eye contact. However, there is also a whole bunch of information that is being shared energetically, which may not be expressed verbally in the conversation. This unconscious energy contains thought forms, emotions, and perceptions of reality. These unconscious energies usually have some affect on where the conversation is going and the general output of energy the person is creating. Much of the intensity is being exchanged energetically without you even realizing it. This is why at times you can walk away from a conversation feeling exhausted, or carrying around a weird thought or perception after being with them. This is mostly noticeable when you walk away and you notice thoughts that you would not normally be thinking. This is a clear sign that you picked them up in your energy field while being with this person or from the environment you were in.

Have you ever been to a sports match and walked in feeling rather subdued, only to return after the event, full of adrenalin and excitement. This is the affect of the collective consciousness emitting a certain frequency of information, which then transformed your frequency.

By choosing to be aware of the field that you share with others, you are able to make decisions for creating a reality that best suits your desire. Conversely, if you are unaware of the energy field, you may walk away thinking that those beliefs, emotions, or perceptions running through your mind are yours. If we are unaware that we are always sharing information, then it's a lot harder to let go of negative patterns when we pick them up in the field. The reason for this is that by not recognizing the information we are picking up, we often make mistake of thinking it is our own belief. Since all beliefs (whether positive or negative) are an illusion then we should be careful upon choosing the ones we live with. If you find yourself in a situation with someone who is processing a lot of denser thought forms, then it's time to really be on your game. You will have to be super alert not to allow their strong belief change your positive viewpoint of reality.

The best thing to do in these situations is rather than trying to give them advice, give them extreme presence. Don't let yourself move into a space of accepting their illusion. Just be present and say very little because ultimately it's your supreme presence that has the power to shift someone's consciousness. At times we often think that it's best to offer an optimistic viewpoint. This can sometimes be very helpful and may give them a new way of seeing the situation. But if we remember that all thoughts are based on illusion and that underneath all illusion is supreme presence and oneness. Wouldn't it be far more affective to hit them with complete truth rather than trying to convince them? This truth has no words. It is a field of knowing your oneness and it has the ability to shift the consciousness of everything around you.

In offering someone a new viewpoint, 80% of the time I would say the viewpoint goes in one ear and out the other. The reason for this is because you are challenging their programming and it can very hard to change someone's programming to another set of beliefs, especially in just one sitting. However, holding supreme presence allows them to see a reflection of who they truly are. This takes no convincing because underneath all of our programs and beliefs is the same field of awareness, which is unity and deep presence. So by shinning this deep presence back at them, you allow them to tune back into the same frequency.

Practicing Supreme Presence

The following is an exercise you can do while supporting someone through a challenge in their life.

Step 1

Before entering the home, center yourself by imagining a connection of lines leading from your feet to the core of mother earth. At the same time, imagine a cord connecting you the stars above. This simple visioning technique keeps your whole energy field in alignment, so it's not pulled off in different directions from outside influences.

Step 2

Still your mind through simple meditation and place an intention to carry the presence with you where ever you go.

Step 3

Upon entering the house and hearing the troubles of your friend, place yourself in deep presence and stillness (non-reactive mode). This lets your friend feel that you're listening but not being swept away in the drama.

Step 4

When your friend presents viewpoints that are destructive, rather than trying to change their viewpoint or encourage it, be quiet and let them keep talking until they have nothing more to say. Usually at this stage, your friend will look to you for some type of response. This can be the hardest part of the task because your ego naturally wants to continue the flow of energy by agreeing with them. But what's most important is that energy is returned to presence. Your silence is going to be a lot more effective than anything else.

Step 5

If he/she feels comfortable, place your hand on their heart and their back and feel the presence and stillness from which you're holding and sharing with her field. You can also do this technique by gazing into their eyes. This eye gazing technique is also a great way to remind them of presence. Ask your friend if it s okay to practice this eye gazing technique. Initially, the person you are working with may feel uncomfortable because they are staring presence right in the face and their ego will want to hide from it so that it can continue to live out its drama. By moving through any uncomfortable feelings with the eye contact, there will be a greater power to shift their consciousness back into presence.

Step 6

When the person is able to feel more present, then naturally the wisdom they are looking for will be found. When the mind is busy creating stories and jumping back and fourth between ideas and perceptions, it is hard to tell when wisdom is found. So by bringing this space of presence wherever you go, you naturally remind people of the presence within themselves, which they always have access to. This is also a great tool because in doing this, you are reminding the person that they are capable of finding all their own answers which allows them to move into a greater state of empowerment for life.

Expansion has no end

As we evolve and start to remember our true connection to unity, our ability to expand into new possibilities and potential becomes endless. Unfortunately, most the people in this world spend their life on a roller coaster of ups and downs. Sometimes they feel really expansive and others painfully contracted. The reason is because they are allowing their feeling and their state of consciousness to be dependent upon their circumstances. So if their circumstances don't appear to be rosy on the surface, they start to contract. On the other hand, when the surface seems peachy clean they are expanding. When someone places their happiness on the surface of life, then the swinging highs and lows of contraction and expansion will continue to appear. As the communion with our true nature becomes the flow of our day (which is unity), then the ability to continue a flow of expansion has no end because we recognize that everything is potential and we are not fearful of trying new things. There is a new mindset, which I invite you to experience and it is this "if I try something new and it doesn't work out, it will not affect my connection to unity". By practicing this new mind set our fear can be placed on the sidelines. By trying new things, we automatically place ourselves in the best position for personal growth and all growth is the process of expansion.

Stepping out of our comfort zones

Change is always upon us and when we allow change to move through our lives without holding onto the past, we can set ourselves up for massive expansion. The number one reason why people don't expand is because of their fear of what will happen if they do. When people are in a place of fearing the unknown, they are placing their identity on the reality of the ego and the ego is always fearful of death. Death means the changing of our identity. But the truth is, our identity will always change as long as we are committed to growth. Our interests may change, the people we have in our life, the way we approach different challenges and the way we see the world. If we allow ourselves to connect to our unity consciousness every day, we will recognize that it doesn't matter what identity is being projected on the surface. The reason for this is, that when our life is fueled by unity consciousness our natural impulse for growth, will always bring to us a perfect expression.

Moving beyond identity

As we move beyond identity, we start to realize that what others think of us no longer matters because we are so comfortable within the knowingness of ourselves. A profound realization occurs in this process that shows you any thought someone has of you is also a projection of their own consciousness and their own identity. That is because when you are coming from a place of unity, you are able to see the surface of all reality simply as a projection of images and games. In seeing this, you realize that these are illusions and are always changing. The one thing that stays the same within everyone is the unity.

Unity consciousness

Unity consciousness is then reflected in all things and a deep feeling of love is felt for everyone as you see your unity in them regardless of what they are projecting upon you. You may be with a friend and they are really angry with you and are accusing you of talking behind their back, which you did not do. In the process of this confrontation, they are throwing all sorts of angry pictures on you through their thoughts. These may include "you are an asshole, you are rude, you are inconsiderate, you are evil etc." All these thoughts are pictures that the person is projecting upon you. If you were in a place of the ego, you may get offended or even start questioning your own integrity, but if you were in a place of unity, you would see the situation for what it really is. Unity consciousness allows you to see beneath the veil and connect into everyone else's unity. So rather than being offended, you notice what levels of illusion and fear this person is carrying around, which has nothing to do with you. In this we discover that the fear that the people carry around has to do with their own ego being threatened.

Abundant eternal universe

Everyone on the planet is going through a cleansing of illusion. Many people cleanse themselves of one illusion on one day, only to pick up a new one the next day! I call this identity jumping. Have you ever known someone who changes his or her name frequently? Maybe even their style, image, or way of life? This act in itself is moving from one illusion to the next. There is nothing wrong with this since we are living in a physical dimension, this can be seen as acts of creativity. Yet the problem arises when a person is not making empowered movements in discovering the truth of their true nature. Instead, they keep layering themselves with more and more projections, seeking safety in layers rather than safety in truth.

After trying on so many suits, ties, and dresses (identities) in my own life, I finally came to a place where I was tired of jumping around so much, and just wished to live in the simple truth. This is when the ultimate surrender of all identities comes into play. This is the dedication to your own inner truth, which is actually the truth of the whole. This is a place of sincerity, where fashion is no longer a place of ego, but rather a creative space to express yourself. The surrender of all identities created by the ego, allows you to move into a place of contentment and peace beyond any pleasure of the outside world.

One may think that if we all resided in unity consciousness, then would we not all look the same, dress the same, and talk the same? I believe one of the most powerful qualities of unity consciousness is pure acceptance of the whole, no matter what form it takes and when this occurs, true creativity springs forth. No longer are we following a projected reality. We are allowing the eternal spring of creation to move through us in the most abundant ways! Life is a celebration and as a result, individuals feel free to express themselves in a unique way.

It all starts with you and as soon as you stop judging other people (or projecting illusion upon other people), is the moment you will start to fully accepting yourself. And what could be better than fully accepting yourself just as you are!

Chapter 5

Cycles of Karma in the Maya

Karma

There are so many thoughts and beliefs in the world about what karma is and how it operates. Many people think karma is cruel. Others believe it to be rightfully just. But I believe both of these opinions take away the simplicity and truth of how karma operates. During this chapter, I am going to break it down in simple terms, to help you understand that karma is simply a process to gain more awareness.

The process of awareness

As we have already discussed, we are moving from a world based on illusion and waking up to our true state, which is unity consciousness. In order to remember that we are truly unified by all things, awareness needs to occur. In today's world, many people are so lost in the illusion that they are creating their world based on only illusion and ego. This can send them into actions of fear, deceit, mistrust, and deception. We need to remember that the only reason people behave in such a way is because they have forgotten their unity with all things and the natural order of the abundant, eternal universe all around them. But in this state, people practice very little awareness as they are continually reacting to their fears, thoughts, and perceptions. So let's say Bob, who just so happens to be deeply lost in the Maya, has found himself in a game of murder. The reasons for his actions are, in his mind, a matter of survival. His family is very poor and one murder would give him enough money to move his family to a better country and hence he decided it was the best thing to do. (Yes, I know it is an extreme case, but I believe extremities are a good place to start).

As we look at Bob's reason for killing another human being, we see that the thoughts and beliefs in his mind told him that it was the right thing to do (maybe Bob thought that the person he was killing was a bad person anyway, so it didn't matter). No matter what Bob believes to be true, this is a projection of his programming. In receipt of doing his job, Bob is able to move his family across to another country, still believing that it was all for the best.

Was Bob's choice based in unity consciousness?

When a decision is made out of knowing your true unity to everything, then all of life is considered because the honoring of all life is present. When Bob made his decision to kill another human being, his decision did not come from a place of honoring the true unity in all things. It came from a place of judgment and ulterior motive. Perhaps he judged that the person deserved it and had also made an agreement to receive a great deal of money out of committing the murder. Any decision that is made from an agreement with the illusion will eventually surface into the consciousness. The reason for this is that at this stage of Bob's life, although he is unaware of his unity, his unity is still there. Just because Bob is unaware of unity consciousness, does not mean it doesn't exist inside of him. The unawareness of Bob's unity through this action of killing another human being (without their consent) will stay with him until he's able to unravel the illusion of the story and once again return to unity.

During times when we place an action into the field around us that is disconnected from our true unity, there becomes a block to recognizing our error. This block comes from the ego and the belief that it was the right thing to do. This belief is only a layer of illusion, which is making us unconscious (or unaware) to our truth.

This unconscious story is then stored in our field until we are able to find the time and space to look at it. However, if we continue to live through the illusion without reflecting on it, then the vibration pattern of this unconscious thought will stay with you.

Now imagine there are two sides to your reality now:
Conscious & Unconscious

The fully conscious part of you knows unity and considers all life when making decisions. The unconscious part is unaware of unity and makes decisions based on fear. However, when the unconscious part becomes conscious, we are able to resolve any actions or wrong doings we have created in the past.

What makes the unconscious becomes conscious?

There are two ways to create more conscious awareness in your life. The first way is through awareness techniques such as meditation, contemplation, yoga, and other exercises that connect you to the feelings of unity. The other way to become conscious is through experiencing pain. When someone experiences large amounts of pain, they are often forced to look within to find why they are experiencing challenges in their life. This internal reflection can make them consider things that they have done to others in the past or may make them rethink the way they see reality.

"Bad" Karma is a process of waking up the unconscious

Let us imagine for a moment that Bob continues to 'believe' that his unconscious act of murdering another human being was the right thing to do (even though in his pure consciousness he is aware that it was not a unified decision, it was selfish and came from the ego). This presents a conflict in Bob's total consciousness because there is an inner divergence between right and wrong – Conscious and Unconscious. When I say right and wrong, all I am referring to is the difference between choosing your actions based on true wisdom and integration with unity consciousness or acting based on the illusion.

Since your true nature will never go away (which is pure consciousness and unity to all things), anything that is not connected to unity will continue to push its way to the surface, until it is resolved. If there is a whole bunch of junk (unconscious programs) blocking you from reaching the surface (unity consciousness), it's going to create a lot of turmoil inside of you. The reason for this is; in order to become fully conscious and aware again, a person must look at all of their belief systems and projections that have been disconnected from unity consciousness.

This can bring up all sorts of chaos because when a person fears looking inside, they may continue to create more disconnection in the outside world.

This creates more and more layers of identity and the more they protect their identity, the more solid they become inside. Since unconditional love is the ultimate expression of oneness and unity consciousness, you can see these types of people become totally disconnected from their heart.

The law of attraction

For anyone who has studied the many teaching that come from the hit documentary "The Secret", you may have a brief understanding that your thoughts create your reality. What I believe is important to focus on in this lesson is that it's not only the thoughts on the surface of your mind, but more potently it is the thoughts coming from your unconscious mind. These are thoughts, which you are not aware of – that are creating your reality.

The process of the law of attraction

The law of attraction tells us that whatever thoughts you have (conscious & unconscious) carry a certain vibration. As discussed earlier, all vibrations hold different information. This information works like a magnet. Since your total vibration equates to your reality, whatever appears on the surface is always a reflection of your internal reality.

Your consciousness is always working to tell you what thoughts; beliefs, patterns, and conditioning you are creating in your world. When we are able to step into a place of empowerment, we are able to look at our reality. We can take responsibility and see what is not working in unison, and clear the patterns in our unconscious mind so that the reality changes. If we are unable to reflect upon our reality, and take responsibility, then we start to play the role of victim believing that the reason we are out of harmony is because of everyone around us, and everything that is happening to us. This propels our current story forward and only continues the illusion, creating more discomfort and chaos in the field.

How does karma relate to the law of attraction?

Whatever is occurring in our reality is a projection of the consciousness we hold. "Bad" karma is simply an expression of those unconscious beliefs, programs, and the conditioning that separate us from our truth and unity. It arises in our world to show us that there is a disconnection from our true source. Many people may look at disease, death, losing a job, breaking a leg, bad finances or any other uncomfortable situation as bad karma. When in fact it is a part of the law of attraction that is designed to wake you up out of the illusion you have created in the first place.

When things manifest in the physical, it has taken a lot of energy to move it there. This is the same way a disease is created in the body. First, there might be a disconnection in your emotional field. Then if you're not connected to it, it might propel you into further disconnection in the mental field. If at that point it's still not heard, it will manifest itself in the physical body.

If there are challenges appearing in your physical world (whether that be through your body, or through the events and relationships you hold) you can guarantee that it has come from an unconscious place within your energy system and ultimately your belief about reality.

Many people will say that these challenges come from past lives and that they accumulate over the ages for you to live out and resolve in the future. I would prescribe to this knowledge. However, for those of you who do not want to delve into the belief of past lives, it Is not necessary. Since all information is locked into the now, it does not matter where the information came from. It might have been another lifetime or it may have come from earlier on in this life.

Regardless of where this information and conditioning came from, all we need to recognize is that it's here now. By placing our awareness and attention on the now, we can move it back into unity consciousness. I believe many people have become delusional with karma and past lives, getting swept away in the stories and the tales of all the identities they once were. This can side track someone from tapping into his or her truth, which is the awareness of now. After all, the projection of an identity is nothing but an illusion in the Maya anyway, and we are deciding to step out of the illusion altogether.

Healing 'karma"

I find it funny to use the word karma, since there are so many layers of belief around this one word. Hopefully, now that we have an understanding of the simplicity around karma, we are able to shift anything in our world from being a challenge to being abundantly fulfilling. The healing of karma is basically the remembering of unity consciousness. When we are able to return all unconscious thoughts of the illusion back into true unity with source, then all of our thoughts and beliefs return to a higher order. When our thoughts become awakened to true consciousness, the law of attraction creates a new reality based on this consciousness.

If you experience a lot of disconnection in your reality, like challenges, it is going to take you conscious awareness and practice to awaken yourself to true knowingness of your unity. Since we live in a world based on illusion, it can be easy to get swept away in the many games and projections people play. The stronger we get within ourselves, the easier it is to walk through life unaffected by drama and co-creating with our own inner magic.

Stepping into the awareness of your own reality

The following is an exercise you can do to see what reality your current state of consciousness is creating. Choose an area of your life that is currently creating a challenge for you. Now complete the following exercise and it will lead you to an awareness of what it is that's creating this problem.

1. What is the challenge?

2. Describe what it looks like and how it makes you feel.

3. When you think of this challenge, what thoughts do you have about it and what is your viewpoint on the challenge?

4. Is this viewpoint connected to solving the problem (move to 5) or being a victim of the problem (move to 4a)?

4a. If the viewpoint is from being a victim, who is it that you blame for the problem?

4b. Why do you blame the person or situation for the problem?

4c. What thoughts do you have about the person or situation who you believe created the problem?

4d. How do these thoughts about this person/situation make you feel?

4e. Do these thoughts contribute to your healing or does it create more discomfort for you?

4f. Do you wish to heal the problem? (move to 5)

When taking responsibility for the problem regardless if you believe it's your fault or not, you automatically shift your beliefs and therefore your vibration into a space of healing and change. By remaining in a state of victim, you are never able to create change. That's because change would be dependent on the outside person or situation changing or apologizing. For that, you could wait a lifetime. So now that you're committed to solving the problem, move to question 5.

5. If you could change the situation, what would it look like?

6. Write down on a separate piece of paper, any thoughts that jump into your head that could potentially be blocking you from transforming the situation. This could include limited beliefs about the situation, inadequate viewpoints on the situation, or negative thoughts about yourself or others.

After writing down as many ideas as you can, reflect on them and see which ones stand out the most. There may be one or many that stand out. Take note and circle the ones that seem to grab your attention. This is part of the process of tuning into your inner intelligence. Some pieces of information may stick with you more than others, so these are the factors to work on.

7. Now that you've found the potential belief patterns that are creating this reality. Place each one neatly on one side of the page and write an action that you could put in place to counteract each limited thought.

Sample Exercise:

My Challenge: Trouble manifesting the perfect job
This makes me feel helpless and depressed

Solving the problem

The situation would be changed by me fully living my dream, dedicated 110%, committing all my extra time to making it happen and being in tune to receiving all the opportunities which are around me, opening myself up to receive.

- I am not ready
- I do not deserve
- My friends do not support my vision and stop the progress
- I feel exhausted as am trying too hard
- Nothing seems to work
- I have always been a failure, why would it change now.

THOUGHT	NEW ACTION
I am not ready	Take one new step every day towards your goal.
I do not deserve	Love myself more every day by writing affirmations for myself.
My friends don't support me	Spend time with friends who love and support me.
I feel exhausted	Go for a walk in the sunshine or do an activity I enjoy.
I have always been a failure	Write down all the times each day that I have been successful & deciding to take note of my success.

Now that you have a new set of action steps, you should post them on your wall. There is no need to post the limited beliefs on the wall, just post the new actions and look at them every day before you get started.

In cases of illness and disease, the exercise above may look different. But it is still important to always remember that whatever is appearing in your energy field as a block is an unconscious program that lacks unity to the greater whole. So if there is a physical discomfort, do the same exercise and find the emotions and thought patterns that come up in your life. Most likely the physical block will also reflect a behavioral or relationship block, either with yourself or those around you.

Rebirth into illusion

Since we currently live our life through linear time, we have a tendency to either live in the past or we live in a projection of the future. What about the now? The illusion is that there is a past and future, when in reality, the only element that truly gives life is the state of our being now. If we are carrying a whole bunch of information and projections from the past, it's very hard to be in the present. When we are reacting to our belief and projections of the past, we tend to project fears and plans into the future. In this current dimension, life in the now is very rarely experienced. However, we do get wind of it. One example would be when a basketball player aims for the hoop and scores. Another is when you go to see your favorite band and they play your choice song. You are so enveloped in the song that no one else exists. Another example is when you are kissing your partner and there is no other feeling than that the love you share in that moment. All of these moments are expressions of truly being in the now. During these times, your attention is not diverted from your task, and the bliss from this space awakens you into the greatest feelings of clarity and presence.

But when the kiss over, or the hoop has been made, we often return to the illusion of past and future. It is very hard for the human mind to fathom the fact that it is only our consciousness creating past and future.

Allowing universal intelligence to direct our life

Due to being caught in the illusion and losing our connection to unity, we have lost our trust in a higher intelligence. We have become identified by ego and the struggles of the ego and the fears that the ego brings along with it. By surrendering the ego, we're able to let go of the projections of where we believe we are in the now. Instead we move into a deep place of trust and allow the now to unfold continually.

There is a difference between being lazy and letting the universe guide you. Both require little effort but one requires awareness. Being lazy comes from a place of feeling unsupported, thereby giving up on living. Allowing the universe to be your guide also requires giving up, but this is a different type of giving up. It's the giving up of the ego, which is the need to control. This then allows you to step into a true place of wisdom (universal wisdom). This is the place where we first came from, where all information exists.

Many people talk about synchronicities in life, where you were just thinking of someone and then they call you – or you are walking down the street and randomly bump into the person you have wanted to talk to. These are all moments of universal intelligence. Why? This is because there was an intuitive part of yourself that directed you there, (regardless of whether you knew it or not). The next step beyond random synchronicities is seeing the correlation between all events and all people and following your feelings wherever you go. The following steps are the three levels that a person goes through in becoming connected to universal intelligence.

Level 1: Unaware & In Chaos

This person is so caught up in the illusion that they are continuously reacting to their conditions and beliefs. Fear is the undercurrent of their life. It moves them into challenging situations, playing the victim and riding the continual rollercoaster of up and down. This person does not believe in synchronicity, even if it jumped out in front of them. This person often finds it hard to be thankful, since they always feel that there is someone else to blame.

Level 2: Awareness in the Illusion

This person has come to a level in their journey where they recognize that they are responsible for much of their reality. At times they may be caught in the illusion. While at other times totally aware of the synchronicities that are making up their life. At times they may be on the rollercoaster, yet they are starting to find ways to tap into synchronicity and understand their true potential and power.

Level 3: Synchronicity is their Natural State

This is the state that we all wish we could be in every moment. The person living in this state is in the deepest state of surrender and trust with the greater universe. They have developed their tools to such an extent that they can tap into synchronicity whenever they like and join the flow of the highest order in the universe. This person feels nothing but gratitude for all of their life – a profound presence and depth is felt when these people are around. This person also feels great comfort in the now, knowing that everything is being looked after as they follow the signs and listen to their intuition.

You may find that you linger between different states of consciousness, sometimes more in the green and other times the red. This is the awakening we all go through as we re-remember our true nature and connection to the greater intelligence.

Chapter 6

Stepping out of the Illusion

The beautiful element to being human is that we all have a choice about how we perceive reality and feel about life. There is a great quote that says "perception is reality" and I find a lot of truth in it. Since you could be living under a dumpster and enjoying life or living in a five story mansion and hate life. Perception is reality. But there is something even greater than perception and that's the feeling of oneness. There is no projection or perception of what oneness is. It is just a feeling of unity, not controlled by a thought. It is living in its natural state without judgment. You may notice the moment you start moving into judgment about something or someone is the same moment you start to feel uncomfortable. That is because you are putting conditions on your reality. Oneness doesn't create conditions; instead it accepts everything as it is.

What I'm proposing to you is instead of choosing which reality you want, choose your state of consciousness – unity or separation. I believe that our world has spent so much time choosing separation–that I honestly believe that we have "been there, done that!" How about changing the choice? Let's choose unity consciousness. We have the choice. We have the tools and we currently live in a time where we can have the freedom to live in unity.

We have been through our fair share of dark times in our planets history, from wars to dictatorships, hierarchies crumbling and falling, religions preaching separation, people starving, forests being destroyed, people dying from diseases that can be cured, fighting over money and resources, animals being killed for the belief that we need meat to survive, our water ways being polluted, our air being tainted, and our supply to the natural life being threatened. All of these realities have been born from a place of separation and ego – a lack of connection to unity.

If we were to wake up and realize that all life can work together, harmonize as one, and be abundant for all, would you join in? Of course you would! But what is it that stops us from realizing this? It is our lack of connection to our individual truth. Our unity connects us to all things and brings out the most compassionate side to our nature. We do have a choice and it's right now. We stand on the brink of change from one way of life to the next. Do we choose to continue to destroy life, its people, the environment, the animals, and the beauty that's moving into life everywhere or do we recognize an opportunity for growth – an opportunity to look deeply within ourselves and find forgiveness and move into a new space of true knowingness of our unity and love to all creation?

The choice is for every individual and that includes you. You can't expect your governments or world leaders to create the change you want to see. It has to start with you. As Mahatma Gandhi once said, "Be the change you wish to see in the world!" Many people are looking outside themselves for the change and in doing so, playing the victim role by saying "George Bush created the war" or "It's their fault, not mine". Whatever blame you are projecting onto the world and its current affairs is a reflection of your disconnection to unity. If you were truly aware of your unity to all things, you would recognize that it's not one person or one thing that makes the world look like it does. Rather it's our collective consciousness and our collective belief on how we view the world that makes it behave in such a way. So by shifting yourself into greater knowingness of your true unity, your role as a messenger will be heard and your message will uniquely correlate to all your gifts and your highest truth of unity. These are the choices you get to make:

Choice one: The Maya

In this beloved choice, you get to move through the world of pictures and projections. The role you play will be dependent upon the family, culture, religion, and country you are born into. This will give you a set of rules to follow that are called beliefs. These beliefs will continually create your role and identity in life and your life will be projected forward through these beliefs and the events that occur from this set of beliefs. At times you may feel conflicted, yet your role will always guide you and this will be your identity. There may be many ups but there are just as many downs in this life. The ups will depend on what you are getting out of life and the downs will depend upon what you feel you are not getting. You will be born into a system that doesn't always agree with you, but you will play your role. Perhaps in following this system, you may receive status and recognition for your agreements in the illusion. You may also face the risk of suffering from illness, which is born out of the illusion as well. At times, you may experience large emotions. While at other times, you may feel numb from emotion all together. These are all choices that will occur in the Maya. Should you choose this life, good luck and we'll see you on the other side!

Choice two: Unity

Your other choice is to be born into the Maya with the intent to practice unity. This is a rare opportunity for a soul because this choice only comes around every 250,000 years and yours just happens to be this lucky year. Otherwise, we would be giving you the choice between Maya or Maya. Interesting selection! However, since Unity is a choice in this day and age, here's how the game would work. You would be born into the Maya, a world based on illusion, projections, pictures, and a linear timeline connected to past and future projections. This world will seem odd to you since you come to the table with a larger understanding of unity. You will witness the world behaving in ways that are out of alignment with your highest truth and it will take courage to live the life you know serves you and the world best. Many times, the Maya may try to change your mind and get you to swap teams. But you are committed to unity. In this commitment, you will set out in finding the tools to maintain your connection to unity. They may include certain exercises such as connection to the breath, meditation, nutrition, and esoteric studies of energy and working in a role that assists other beings, supporting the environment, or bringing a message of transformation through your work. You may also look upon those around you who are in the Maya and assist others in teaching them tools and techniques to living in unity consciousness. The role of unity may be just as hard as the world in the Maya, since there will be many influences hoping to change your state of harmony. Yet, if you commit to unity, the fulfillment and rewards will be far more beneficial than any material possession you can receive in the Maya. Should you choose unity, you will always be connected to other planes of consciousness outside of the physical realm. Your intuitive capabilities and natural intuition will guide you home whenever you need it and the support of the greater universe will always be on your side.

Many of us are at a stage of our life where we are now realizing this choice is available. Some of us have been living a world solidly based on illusion and by reading this book may be given an insight into your true nature. No matter where you are in waking up to this beautiful truth within, you are on the right track. Be patient with yourself because this is the most beautiful realization you may ever have in your life – the power to choose between unity and illusion. When we start making choices based on unity, we will start to see a different order take place. It's important to take your time, yet make it your intention to look at every part of your life – from the relationships you live in, to the work you do, and even the food you eat, the attitudes you have towards others, the beliefs you have about yourself, the habits you practice, and the way you treat your environment and those around you. This is a life-long project, yet every step of the way brings new clarity and understanding. Every moment you challenge an old belief is a moment you allow yourself to step into eternity and feel your truth. So keep moving forward.

The following are some steps when deciding to move into Unity Consciousness. You can apply each step to every part of your life.

Releasing Filters

This is the process of moving all your thoughts, feelings, attitudes, and beliefs back into a space of love and unity. A great idea is to carry a small diary around with you and take note of any filters that you feel are disconnecting you from love. Write down the filters and then as mentioned in chapter five, work at releasing them by creating actions that counteract that belief. You can also release filters by going into them deeply, finding where it came from, and recognizing that it came from an illusion or a story of pain. Maybe someone told you to think that way, or something occurred in your life that made you perceive reality in that light. By going back into the place where you first picked it up, you are able to shift the viewpoint of it.

Cleaning up the emotional body

Start to become aware of the buttons that push you into emotional spew. Every person usually carries a few buttons that when pressed will make you fly off the handle and turn into the wicked witch of the west or the evil dragon from down south! If you are able to become aware of your emotional buttons, you are able to watch them closely. By becoming aware of what makes you snap, you're able to become aware of your insecurities and thus move them back into love. If we do not bring attention to our own buttons, then we will continually think it is every one else's fault around you. Be patient with yourself. But every time you feel your button being pressed, take a breath before reacting and ask yourself, "Am I playing victim right now and does this emotion serve me and my health?"

Align the mind

The mind often carries many limited belief patterns about reality, and carrying around all that junk can stop your mind from working at its highest potential. By releasing the filters, your beliefs and judgments will soon move away. Then it is up to you to fill your mind up with positive thoughts and harmonize the frequency to patterns of higher order and outlook. It is absolutely imperative to cleanse the filters in order to make this part of the exercise successful. The reason is because if there's no room in the brain to create new patterns then new patterns will not be created. Upon cleansing the filters, decide to harmonize your brain waves through synchronized music. There are specific patterns of music that allow the brain to harmonize alertness, greater awareness, and clarity. Many classical tracks such as Mozart work with this particular technique. This is why parents are always told to play classical music to their unborn child while in the womb – because the child's brain is supple and will harmonize to the intelligence of the harmonics played in the music. Upon releasing filters, do activities that inspire your creativity or enthusiasm. Painting, singing, and playing sports are all great examples. All of these activities bring joy allow and release happy endorphins and serotonin, which set your brain up for a new type of chemistry!

Cleansing the body temple

This is one of the most important ingredients to moving you into an ultimate state of health after being lost in the illusion for so many years. The body is an expression of all the beliefs you carry around – both conscious and unconscious. In my process of cleansing, I've realized that it is not as simple as taking a detox box of herbs for a week and thinking you are clean. There is a definite process you want to go through in order to clean up the body to the state it deserves. Remember that no matter how old you are, the longer you have been putting harmful substances, toxins, emotions, and thoughts into your body, the more time you will have to spend in bringing yourself back to balance. As you work on cleansing your body, you may notice that old memories and emotions start to emerge. This part of the cleansing process should be taken slowly. You can commence by cleansing organ by organ. In ancient studies such as Chinese medicine, it is understood that each organ contains a different emotion. So don't be surprised if through the cleansing process, specific emotions may resurface as each organ becomes purified. As you clean the body, the emotional memories and programs connected to your body will lessen and have less control over the behavioral patterns in your life.

Shifting your diet

Part of stepping into unity is honoring everything that goes into your body. As you develop a new relationship with the rest of body, mind and spirit, you might notice your cravings and desires for certain foods to lessen. That's because certain foods usually relate to certain emotional habits and addictions. This is why emotional eating becomes a destructive pattern for individuals suffering from depression and anxiety. As you reconsider the way you view food, I would take into account the position of unity consciousness. That way anything you put in your body comes from a place of knowing true unity and compassion. Aside from the fact that meat is very hard to break down in the body, you're also placing the adrenalin and the fear of the animal when consuming the meat. It's a very inhumane act and does not take into the account the unity of all life and the right for all creatures to live the life it deserves. This can be a very controversial topic, which is why I like to point people directly to the facts on how damaging meat and meat products is for the health of the body temple. There is a lot of misinformation in the world about diet and health; many people profess to know the hidden secrets of ageless vitality. The best information I have come across are two of my favorite teachers and authors Dr. Shawn Miller and David Carmos who have written multiple books on health and nutrition, one of them being "You are never to old, to become young". This book will guide you through the steps of transitioning your diet to a new way of vitality without shocking the system.

Another note I would like to make, since diet has changed my life so much, if you start placing more living foods into your body you will notice a new bounce to life. The reason for this is you're putting life into your body and not death. Do you want your body to be a tombstone for dead animals or do you want it to be an Amazon forest filled with healthy bacteria and vibrating life. Just in the same way that your thoughts create your reality, whatever food you put in your body holds information and this will also impact your reality and the way you see life. So choose wisely what goes into that temple of yours and choose only the highest vibrations. You are what you eat.

Being true to yourself

One of the most important ingredients I would recommend when shifting your life to choice number 2 (unity consciousness) is the commitment to yourself. Often, when we make changes in our lives, the people around us will be the first to let us know they have a problem with it. The reason is that they fear if you change, your love for them will also change or the control they used to have over you will shift. Almost all negative reactions people make towards your new zest for life will potentially make you want to crawl back in that shell you came from. This is the time you have to remain committed to your practice and the new understandings you have of yourself. Don't try to convince people of your change or prove anything to them. The easiest way to stay connected to your truth is by doing it without putting forth too much effort. One of the biggest mistakes most people make when they are going through a life change is trying to impose their new beliefs on everyone around them. This actually creates more resistance from others and can often make your new passion for life fade away fast. Instead, of doing this, decide to remain neutral. Keep a daily routine that allows you to check in with your progress, so that you are not led off track. Soon you will realize that you do not need to say anything to change someone's opinion, because you will be a walking example of new health.

Your daily check-in

Here is an exercise that you can do daily. This will allow you to track your progress as well as remind yourself to continually be true to your new self. Get a diary that you can keep by your bed and before you sleep, answer the following questions:

1. What filters did I cleanse today? And what shifts have I made in my attitude?

2. On a scale of 1 to 10, what was my emotional awareness like today and was there anything that pushed my buttons? What was it and why?

3. How can I perceive the same challenges differently next time?

4. What did I do for my mind today that allowed it to be cleared and stimulated by the full joy and positive vibration of life?

5. If I'm doing a body cleanse, what organ or part of the body did I work on today? Did any emotions come up with this healing? How do I feel after working through this part of the body today?

6. What foods did I choose to eat today and how does my body, mind, and emotions feel after eating this food? Judging by how I feel after eating this food, would there be any changes I could make in the future that would be more suitable for my body and health?

7. I was true to myself today by ……… (fill in the blank).

Identities in the Illusion

As we break free of the layers upon layers of identity, we start to realize that much of the world is communicating through identities and roles. When people are solidly built into the identity they are playing, they commence communicating through that character and believe that is whom they truly are. This can become destructive because after a while, the human element disappears from the person and all that remains is their identity communicating to another identity. What identity do you play in life? Here are a few examples of identities: Mother, father, daughter, son, teacher, student, sick person, celebrity, child, princess, servant, guru, genius, know it all, poor person, life of the party, nun, saint, devil, model, fashion expert, photographer, player, sleaze, etc.

The list of identities goes on and on. Here is the trick to mastering life. You are not these identities; rather they are just something you can do. When you approach these identities without latching your whole life to them, you give yourself permission to move between different roles. This will then give you the liberation to play whatever game you want to when you want to. By trapping yourself into one role, life can become very rigid and boring. For example, you might be playing the role of teacher and your friend may be playing the role of student. Because both of you have become so attached to the role, it becomes impossible to reverse roles because it would hurt your ego. You might like to play the student, as you feel you could also learn from your friend, yet your ego feels embarrassed to admit that you do not know everything. This is the problem when an individual wants to grow through another role. Yet they fear letting their other role down and what people may think of them if they switched roles. By holding onto an identity, you may be stopping your growth. This is why getting in touch with your inner child can be a great way to move between roles.

Chapter 7

The Inner Child

The inner child has no Identity

One of the reasons why children have so much fun and learn so much at a young age is because they are continually changing roles and playing different identities. It is a child's favorite past time to play all these roles. They understand the joy of all expressions and this allows them to move into many different realities. When we are able to experience more than one reality, we are truly able to gather a greater wisdom and understanding for the world and the people around us. This ability to understand more than one reality gives us greater compassion and unity with all things.

Everyone has an inner child

If you are continually attaching yourself to one identity, there will only be a small percentage of people you can relate to because in order for anyone to understand you, they must understand your role and your role must relate to them. For example, if a mother was always playing the role of mother and she went to hang out with her friends and continued to play that role of mother, she would then experience the same reality wherever she went, with her children as well as everyone she interacts with. But what if she chose to play the role of mother when she was looking after her 5-year-old son while playing the role of best friend when she was hanging out with her friends? She would definitely have a more diverse experience of life and learn a lot more from the reality around her.

One ingredient that I find always works in any situation is communicating to the inner child of others. The reason this works so well is everyone person has an inner child inside. Some people's inner child is more free and playful in its environment while other's inner child is tucked safely away, only to reveal itself when feeling secure and protected. The reason for this is that those who hide their inner child were once taught that it was not ok to be open and free. These types of people are the ones who hold themselves close to their chosen identity as protection. Their identity has become their safety net.

In this case, the child inside will only make itself seen in situations of close comfort and people they know well. Maybe with a loved one, a partner, or a best friend, their inner child will come out to play. But at other times, the child hides behind a mask.

If you allow yourself to be innocent, vulnerable, and playful like a child, you automatically give those around you permission to play the same game. This is the best way to break down anyone's walls. Just be free and vulnerable in your truth and they will be comfortable to do the same. Your child is not afraid of making mistakes, nor are you afraid of looking silly or saying the wrong thing. Your inner child only wishes to connect with others and play. There is an opening in the heart that reaches out to the other and says, "Hey, we are on the same team. Let's play!" This signal that you send to others warms them up to play and takes the seriousness out of the identity they have been hanging on to.

If you communicate to people through their identity, then you are re-enforcing that identity in them. Of course, it's wonderful to play different roles but the moment you start seeing that person 'only' in that role is the moment you have fallen for the illusion. No one is one thing, we are everything and we are always growing in everything also. For the teacher may have a lot of wisdom, but if they stop learning because they think they know everything, then pretty soon the student will outgrow the teacher. So be aware of the agreements you are making with other peoples identities. If you feel they are becoming solid in their role, focus on bringing out their child and that will loosen them up to play again and expand their horizons.

The qualities of the inner child
- Open
- Flexible
- Gentle

- Vulnerable
- Free
- Playful
- Imaginative
- Loving
- Inspired
- Curious
- Joyful
- The Child Loves to Love

One beautiful quality about children is that they love to love and usually the younger they are, the more they are able to hold that space of love. I'm sure we have all been in a situation, whether riding on the bus or waiting in the grocery store line, where we have noticed a young child being held by mom or dad. As we look upon this young infant, the child looks back at us with great big curious eyes. It is a long trip on the bus or through the line at the grocery store. So the child continues to study all the features on your face – not looking away for over a minute. In the process of this enquiry, you become delighted by the child's curiosity and turn into a child yourself, making silly noises, pulling funny faces, or looking back at the sweet angel as they stare in to your world. There is not a moment that goes by where fear or resistance enters your mind. You simply feel the love from the child and in return reflect the love back. This is a great example of two children connecting freely in the field of awareness together. Instead of being in a state of fear, they decide to play. If this same scenario happened between "adults" then the interpretation of the situation would be a whole lot different and all sorts of perceptions would start flying around in both of their minds. Since the young child has not been trained to judge yet, there are no thoughts or perceptions that the young child is projecting. Rather, the young child is curiously investigating.

Curiosity

Curiosity is the key to allowing your inner child out to play. As mentioned before, the reason for this is that when judgment has been removed, there is an open field for curiosity to play in. The beautiful element of curiosity is that it never gets bored because there is always something new to see, do, and learn. This is due to not separating yourself from the world through the illusion that you have an identity. When you are attached to your identity, your world becomes limited because there are only so many ways to interpret the world around you. When you let down your attachment to an identity, you realize the world around you is large and in that there are many ways to see the world.

Playing in the illusion

When our inner child is open and free, the world of illusion and images become a really fun game. To start with, we are born into this body with 5 senses, eat, taste, touch, hear, and see. These 5 senses alone can stimulate you into ecstasy if you allow it. As adults we have experienced so much in our senses that often it becomes an overload and we either become addicted to it, or numbed to it. The child on the other hand, savors the moments, the sensations and dives deeply into them as if it were the last day in the universe!

Chapter 8

Ascending into Greater Universe

The fabric of consciousness Holds all information

Hopefully by this stage in the book, you can understand through cleansing the walls of perception and maintaining a healthy mind, body, and spirit, we are able to live in a space of unity consciousness. This space of consciousness is expansive and it allows us to move into any space of knowledge we wish to tap into. This is because we have removed any blocks in our identity, which may have stopped us from seeing what was there all along. This means anything that has been created in the field of awareness is available for us to know. This information is not limited to the knowledge of our planet, but the whole cosmos, parallel dimensions, other planets and all realms of consciousness. Since our unity to all things includes the wider cosmos, then it naturally makes sense that we can tune into any information that it holds.

Higher states of consciousness

Much of our reality is based on information pertaining to the physical field and dimension. That is because these are the areas that are mostly observed by the physical eye. This does not mean that these are the only things occurring in reality at the one time. Actually, what we can see with the physical eye is only a microscopic portion of the larger picture. I'll begin to describe some of the many layers I've had access to through my journey into deeper awareness. The levels of seeing go even further into greater dimensions as we open ourselves up, since we live in an infinite reality.

First level of seeing: Astral plane

The Astral Plane that I've had access to seeing from a young age is the next densest level of vibration after the physical vibration. On this field, you'll often see deceased loved ones, entities, and spirits that have not yet moved on from the Earth Plane. These spirits can either be lost and unsure of where they are, and often at times just looking for attention. Or there may be spirits who do not want to move into their next dimension some whom have just left their body and are reviewing their family and friends. The other spirits I have come across are the trickster spirits and they enjoy playing games with humans. I've experienced these trickster spirits many times, mostly at night when I'm in between states of consciousness. Since I have opened my consciousness, I'm often very aware when there is the energy of another spirit in the room. When we are unaware of these beings, we can often be affected by their games and not even realize it. Many times these trickster spirits like to put thoughts and ideas into our mind, which might be damaging to your reality. This is why sometimes, you may be walking down a dark ally and get a really weird idea in your mind, which is totally out of character, like how to commit suicide or break into an unknown house. Luckily for us who have a level of balance in our mind, can witness such thoughts coming through and recognize that they are not our own. However someone who is less stable, may start listening to these thoughts, thinking that they are their own, and follow the lead of these sneaky spirits.

The truth is there are always spirits hanging around in different dimensions. Often, the type of spirits that hang around will reflect the general vibration of the environment and the people who have spent time in it.

The best way to start training yourself for this level of awareness is to feel the energy of a room when you walk into it. It is even better to do this when there is no one else there. That way, you know it's coming from the room. It can also be usual for people to carry these entities around with them without even realizing it.

As you become more aware of energies, you will start seeing colors around people as well as denser, darker patches in people's aura. These can often be entities following people around. These entities follow people around for a lot of different reasons. For the most part, when they are darker energies, it's because they are feeding on your light and are probably enjoying influencing your thoughts and reality.

From a very young age, I was able to see the astral field and many times I would wake up and see spirits in my room. Sometimes they would try to communicate with me. But most of the time, I was so scared that I did not open myself to investigating the field. When I turned 17, I began moving into an unhealthy time of my life, which lasted for about three years. Like many curious teenagers, I began taking party drugs, eating unhealthy foods and having very little sleep. I later realized, the reason why I had these habits was due to my unconscious and unresolved patterns and thus disconnection to unity consciousness.

During this time, the types of entities I began to see became very different than the ones that sometimes showed up as a kid. These entities were angry and aggressive. They would hiss at me in the night. On one occasion, my astral body was raped by another spirit. It sounds funny that a spirit without a body could rape a person so let me share this experience. I woke up one night in my astral body. My physical body was still asleep, yet the astral body sat up right out of my physical body. Then all of a sudden, I felt this pressure of another being push me back into my body and push my head into the side of the pillow. Then the legs of my astral body were pushed up over my head while this spirit placed its energy in me. During this half dream half reality, I could not move as my head was pushed into the pillow. I could not scream out, even though I tried and my whole physical body felt as though it were being raped.

It is a very weird circumstance to understand for someone who only relates to the physical, 3D world. But as we start to become aware of all these other dimensions happening at once, we start to see how all the dimensions are connected the one dimension. Just because we cannot see it, doesn't mean that it's not happening.

As I mentioned earlier, I've noticed the types of entities or spirits you attract usually reflect your consciousness and state of health. The reason for this is vibration and the law of attraction. Naturally, if your body, mind, and emotions are operating from a muggy place, then you attract other muggy energies to you.

If you are coming from a clear and healthy space of consciousness, you would be aware of something muggy hanging out in the field because it would not resonate with your general state of being. Therefore, you would recognize that it's not you but rather something else in the field creating those vibrations and it would have no control over you.

Nature Spirits

In the process of cleansing the walls of perception, other realms that have also emerged from our physical realm become present. If you are an outdoor person and enjoy the environment, you may feel a great oneness with the nature around you. It is usually the times when we have a quieter mind that this oneness feeling unfolds in nature. If you have ever been out for a hike and had a lot on your mind, you may have noticed that the experience would have been different if you were more relaxed. The reason for this is that you are more open to receiving the magnificence of everything around you when you are relaxed. Whereas when you are thinking a lot, your attention moves from expanded awareness to inner dialogue. When experiencing stress your awareness may leave a place of seeing the magnificence of everything, such as the colors, the smells, and the geography and instead move you into another world and another dream. The reason I say dream is because when we are going through a lot of inner dialogue, the discussion we are usually having is the projection and perception of past and future. These discussions in your mind are also processed through your filters and past experiences. That is why it is a deep dream, because it is part of your conditioning and belief system.

As we take a moment to connect to the direct environment around us, we're able to connect to the now. This now brings the awakening and awareness of the life around us.

Ascended Masters

Since diving deeper in to my spiritual practice and accessing quieter spaces of stillness, I have been guided into communion with many beings that we may label as ascended masters or teachers in other dimensions. These are often beings that have once lived upon the Earth and have done great work and service while maintaining a high state of consciousness on Earth. Many of these are the great teachers that come from the world religions and ancient traditions such as Jesus, Buddha, Krishna, Quan Yin, Moses, Allah, Lao Tzu and many other saints who left wisdom upon the planet.

The one element that brought all of these ascended masters together was that they were not dogmatic. Although there have been many religions built around their teachings, the one lesson that echoes true which has always been practiced is to love all and cast no judgment.

The ascended masters offer us great teachings and the steps to greater levels of awareness. If the teachings are received from a pure heart, then we have been given the tools to remember our oneness. As we call upon these great masters through prayer, visualization, journaling, or conscious thought we automatically invite their wisdom into our life.

Since we can now understand life is not dependent on the physical body being alive, rather it is the consciousness being present, we can see that by focusing on the consciousness of these great masters, we automatically bring them back into the now. The consciousness and wisdom of these great teachers does not disappear with them when they die. The wisdom remains in the field forever and we are capable of tapping in whenever we wish and drawing upon the great knowledge, which is a part of our own great knowledge.

For many years I've studied the world religions and been inspired by the teachings of these great masters. Through being able to honor the sacred truth in these religions, I have been able to step out of a dogma and rather recognize truth, which many of these teachers are communicating. This has led to greater levels of clarity as I have peeled off the filters of perception in order to commune with these great beings.

One night I was attending a ceremony at a friend's home, and I received a message while attending the toilet. It was an interesting experience as I sat down to pee! I heard a voice telling me that I must return home immediately as there was information that the higher realms wished to share with me. In the process of receiving this message, the whole room had flashed in bright light and I saw two angelic figures in the corner of my eye, one on either side of me.

The reason I believe I received this message was due to my state of consciousness after participating in a fire ceremony. Upon reaching home, I lay myself down only to receive about 5 hours of information on consciousness and duality. This one experience in essence propelled me to write this book. During this experience I was also shown the life of an ascended master, Jesus, and his duty on the planet, along with the process of awakening that each and every soul goes through in order to be elevated from duality consciousness to unity consciousness.

This experience gave me great clarity in understanding the importance of service and how living a life of service is one of the easiest ways to lift a person out of the shackles of illusion and into a higher plane of existence.

A life of service

When we are able to move our focus away from "getting" to "giving", then we naturally open the flood gates to communing in more expansive states of unity. The reason for this is; by giving, you are turning your attention to the outer world, as an extension of yourself. And as you give to others, a level of fulfillment beyond an individual pleasure starts to fill you up. When we are focused on getting, we are actually taking all the energy of the universe and trying to hoard it in a small dimension. We have forgotten that we are a part of the larger creation and as a result, the pleasure cannot be shared. It can only be hoarded, because there is a fear that if you share your pleasure with others, they may take your pleasure away. A prime example is a young child with a bag of lollies who does not want to share with his friend, because he wants all the pleasure to himself. So instead of sharing, he hides away in a corner by himself, eating each and every treat available, making sure his friends does not see. If this same child were to open up and develop a consciousness of service, which is giving, then he may find that by sharing his bag of treats with his friend, he would gain another level of pleasure, which is the heart connection with his friend, the satisfaction of seeing his friend happy, and the joy of sharing. If this young child decided to share with his friend, he may also start to see his world become more expansive as his friend now offers him a bite of his sandwich and his favorite crayon to draw with. As you can see by choosing a life of service, your world begins to expand and in actual fact, you end up getting more than what you have ever asked for.

Chapter 9

The Greater Universe

Did you ever notice a time in your life when you were caught in a misunderstanding? Maybe you were suspecting someone as a liar (although later found out that it was just a story you had in your mind and in fact they were telling the truth).

Think back to this time. This particular scenario starts with one projection. Maybe you notice that something they said was out of line and as the interpretation of their words enter your mind, you start creating stories about what they really meant and then that stories propels you into another story and you start looking at all of their behavior in that light and calculating their past actions and future actions. Before you know it, you have projected so many stories in your mind that have become disconnected from the true connection with the person.

When this occurs and the stories have taken over, your projected belief about this person can be so strong that you find it difficult to approach them about it. This is when communication shuts down and greater levels of separation enter the field. Many friendships, relationships, and families have been broken and separated from this one process alone.

As we become aware of the refractions we carry around in our field, we are able to watch these projections and recognize them as our own belief and program. It is very important that we are aware when it is our own projection verses actual reality.

The best way to tell if it's coming from your projected reality is to ask yourself if what you are seeing makes you feel insecure. When we feel insecure, we are reacting to a part of ourselves that doesn't feel secure. The reason we don't feel secure is because we are carrying around a projection in our field. This projection is what separates us from our truth, which is oneness.

When we are in a true state of oneness, we do not feel insecure about other people's poor habits. We simply recognize that it is part of their refraction in consciousness. In seeing this, we grow in compassion as we only wish for them to feel the wholeness, which we feel. Instead of reacting and creating drama, we hold out our hand to assist.

When the pure consciousness (which is the true state of our being) is able to become aware of itself, time stops and presence is found. The soul holds the template of all experiences that your consciousness has lived. When all of these experiences and pieces of information can be held in presence, all levels of "karma" can be released.

When there is nothing but pure awareness in the now, all thought projections, beliefs, and conditions of the past disappear. Therefore, no longer creating a world of repetitive karma and you are now in a place of supreme intelligence. This is the place of unification with all knowledge. No longer are you defined by the refractions in consciousness. You're aware of everything as one.

This creates a level of deep selflessness because the ego, which was once creating your dream, has now disappeared. So who's creating your dream now? Complete awareness.

This complete awareness is the element within you that watches the game unfold, yet is not identified by the game. A deep presence of knowing that there is no right or wrong, just events and happenings. Many people may think that this energy would be totally disconnected from human connection and love. Yet, it is quite the opposite. This level of complete awareness is so deeply connected to love that it doesn't identify itself but rather comes here to serve the greater whole.

The joys shared and manifested continue to pass us by like a continual spiral into nothingness. The being is completely aware is their eternal self. There's no attachment or need because they realize that they already have everything.

Attachment is what keeps us locked in time and our chosen reality. When attachment arises within us, we are allowing our consciousness to identify with an object. This identification with an object serves as a way to compensate for our place in separation consciousness. For example, Janet is carrying a belief about herself that she is unlovable. And this belief has become so solid in her identity that she very rarely feels at one with the world around her. Instead, as a way to compensate for this state of separation consciousness, she becomes very attached to her lover, believing that by having a partner by her side she can feel at one. In this case, the lover has become an object to support her unconscious belief of not feeling loved or good enough. Yet, this is not true oneness for it is dependent on something outside of her, which ultimately means it is not sustainable. Therefore, when her lover leaves, a sense of separation and fear arises again and the belief of not being loved is once again exposed.

Many people also flip completely the other way. They may be carrying a belief that by being attached, they feel pain. So they create a new belief that in order to not feel pain, they must detach. But this detachment is still based on fear and separation. It just contains another layer. Therefore, the feelings of oneness and unity with all things still do not exist. These kinds of people are often seen as very distant.

True unity consciousness allows a person to be in a deep space of unconditional love. There is no attachment or need to receive anything rather the consciousness allows objects to be presented, shared, and released.

When a person is deeply attached to an object in their mind, whether it be a thought from the past or something they are experiencing in the now, it is hard for them to see the infinite potential and realities existing simultaneously at once. For this level of consciousness says, "That's all I want, and there is nothing else better out there for me." This is a limited viewpoint on reality and in the essence of holding on; they begin to create a reality based on what they want their object to represent. When their object stops giving them their desires or if their object doesn't fulfill their desires, instead of allowing the natural state of the object to exist, the person will begin demanding that their object change so that they can feel whole and fulfilled by it.

Surrender expectation

As we surrender the expectation we have on the various objects in our lives, we move into a place of allowing everything to vibrate in its natural state. This could be a person, place, or thing. This is when we tap into universal flow because we are no longer allowing the ego to control our reality – we are allowing a greater intelligence to move us wherever it wants us to go. This act opens us up to miracles because now there is no expectation, just surprises!

This is a feeling of truly living in the now because expectations are linked to the past and the future. It is created by a belief you picked up in the past and what you feel you deserve. This belief is then projected into the future onto what you believe you should get out of the objects in your life.

Many people say that the best time in a relationship is the honeymoon stage. Love is thriving. There is very little expectation. The couple is simply enjoying the miracles that unfold every day. The moment expectations start to move into a relationship is the moment it starts to degenerate. Because now you're claiming ownership over your object and when the objects don't meet your demands, conflicts arise.

As humanity shifts back into a greater level of oneness, we will definitely start to see relationships along with many other old systems shift and transform into restored harmony. Ultimately, as we reunite with oneness, everything in our outside world will reflect that same state of unity and peace. In order for this to happen, all the refractions in the field must be reconciled so that presence can be found.

As mentioned before, if we look everyone on the planet, we may see many systems of belief that are creating separation. As we learn to witness one another as a reflection of our own consciousness, we are able to take responsibility for our lives and no longer blame, hate, or point the finger at anyone else.

A new world based on light

We are light beings that hold frequencies of energy that contain light. The less conscious and aware a human is, the less light they are emitting into the world around them.

If we think of light as an on switch and darkness as an off switch, we can relate this to fields of being conscious and unconscious. When we are conscious and aware, we are usually 'on', which means to say that there is an alertness within us that allows us to co-create an external reality, which is full of balance or light. This is then reflected in day-to-day life, our relationships, work, friendships, and all activities. When our unconscious patterns are stronger than our conscious patterns, then the external reality around us starts to crumble.

Now imagine we get to change the word conscious for love and unconscious for lack of love. When we are in the full embodiment of love, we experience not only the most harmonizing energy in the universe but also the clarity and vision to assist other people to awaken into their light.

More light inside creates more love

Many ancient traditions from Egyptians, Indians, to ancient tribes across South America refer to cleansing the body and awakening new levels of consciousness through activating "the light body" and what this means to say is, the activation of remembering our deepest connection to love, and union to all of creation. There are many tools and techniques you can use to activate the light body in order to both awaken higher states of consciousness, and bring the shadow of the unconscious into the conscious.

Looking into our darkest places of consciousness does not have to be as scary or frightful as you believe it to be. The idea of looking at an unconscious part of yourself in the past is very scary because it means looking at your fears and who wants to do that? That is why they got buried so long ago.

The activation of the light body allows you to remember your true essence, which is love. Therefore, anything that holds onto the frequency of fear disappears because the illusion of it no longer exists. This occurs simply by knowing that all fear is simply an illusion. By embracing yourself as part of the whole, you are able to see that everything outside of you is a reflection of you and that you have created it. Therefore, you are no longer becoming the victim of circumstance but the knowing creator of circumstance.

The following exercise will assist you in activating your light body. The beautiful thing about this technique is you can use it any time, anywhere. You do not need to go into solitude meditation to practice this exercise, although putting this exercise into use on a daily basis will allow you to remain in a meditative state through all of your activities and connections.

Step 1: Awaken your light body

Imagine that you are the only thing in the universe and that everything you are seeing in your reality, you are creating right now. The words you are reading, you are creating from your own field of awareness and you are creating your whole external environment right now. See how your consciousness is creating this picture right in front of you?

What does the quality of your environment feel like? Are you sitting somewhere in comfort? Do you feel safe? How is the environment affecting you?

As we begin to harmonize more of our inner peace into the environments that appear less peaceful, we are able to change the shape of the environment and move to our next level of consciousness.

You will only move to your next level of consciousness when you are able to harmonize and find peace in the areas of your life that seem difficult. This occurs by choosing to remain in balance instead of reacting and becoming the victim to them. The victim is the state of separation that forgot it was creating its reality, whether that is a happy or sad reality.

When we find peace in these challenging areas, the environment automatically changes and before you know it, you have painted a brand new environment with your consciousness. You are the artist of your destiny.

Step 2: Awaken the light body

Another technique that can be used in activating the light body is choosing to see light in all your perceptions, actions, and reactions. This may be easy in some areas of your life, while in others it may be more challenging. When I say seeing light what I'm referring to is seeing love. The areas in our life where we place judgment are usually the areas that lack the most love. The step that exists between overflowing love and lack of love is the space of acceptance.

108

If you are having trouble finding true, unconditional, overflowing love, then start with acceptance. By accepting another individual for whatever they are or have created in their reality, you allow them to be them. This automatically empowers you to be in control of your own harmony.

There are many times we may feel justified in casting judgment on another. Yet in truth, it's only our lack of awareness that creates this viewpoint. The reason is that judgment only allows you to see part of the story, rather than the whole story. If we allowed ourselves to see the whole story, we would have compassion.

Let's use a serious judgment that I'm sure many people would find difficult in with- the love for a murderer. In order to find compassion for such a person, one must see the totality of the experience. By acknowledging the totality does not make it right, yet you are able to understand the causes, thus be moved to greater compassion.

The following exercise is designed for you to focus on a challenge you may be facing in your life. Perhaps there is a relationship or someone you are finding hard to forgive. For this example I will use the forgiveness of a murderer.

What happened?
An evil man murdered my child.
What is my judgment?
He's an evil man and deserves to rot in hell.
What pain does the other person feel (unconscious or conscious) in their life?
Maybe this person was physiologically, physically, or emotionally abused to a level that created intense internal conflict.
What is that pain of the other person?
Maybe he felt intensely scared, alone, fearful, sad, and anxious.
Can you see how their unconscious emotions and pains created the reality?
Yes.

If you could change anything in this situation so that your daughter was not killed (or write your circumstance) so that everyone involved felt a state of peace, what would you do?
In order to resolve the situation before it happened, I would change the murderer's pain to love so that he would not have committed this act.

What can we do in our individual reality now to create the harmony we desire?
Depending on your place of developed compassion and how deep you are willing to understand, the other person's pain will show what the answer will be. Perhaps one of the following answers may best describe your response.

- I would forgive the other person, as I understand their reality.
- I would assist the other person so that they can heal and this does not happen again.

Both of these answers allow you to take charge of your light body and harmonize your environment. If you are unable to find acceptance for what is, the environment will always look the same and you will be living in hell forever.

Once we recognize that by holding grudges and resentments we are only damaging our own life and then we're able to let them go.

States of consciousness

If we think of God as the energy that unifies everything, then we can see that this is the place from which we came from. Out of this place, we begin to experience separation, yet in truth they are simply different expressions of God (since it all came from God). Within creation, all expressions live. By choosing to submerge ourselves in the various states of separation, we get to fully experience whole-heartedly that one individual expression of God. Just like the colors in the rainbow, we get to experience the many different colors at different times, but ultimately they all belong to the same rainbow. This exercise of experiencing all the unique expressions of the one shows our deepest love, because we have chosen to spend so much time getting to know all the nuances (feelings, emotions, and considerations to that specific frequency of energy). When we have learnt what we need to learn from each expression, we are able to release and merge into another expression or unique identity of the whole.

Doing the soul work

Doing our individual soul work is more important than any other type of work on the planet right now. All other types of work are reflections of our souls conditioning and projections based on the skills we have picked up and the karma we have attributed along the journey. All is a collection of layers upon layers of experiences that have accumulated to create a sense of importance. This is not at all to take away from the rainbow of expressions we have all been gifted with. Instead by doing the soul work, we are able to express these gifts better than we could ever imagine possible.

Yet in order for us to survive as a species, the most important thing in this day and age is to do your inner soul work. This means peeling off the layers of illusion.

As we go deep into peeling the layers, we start to see the tension we have stored in our system. These are unresolved stories in our soul that have been collected and due to the lack of resolve in certain stories life can become quite challenging.

The work is in doing the soul work. That will create your purpose, your message, and the story of highest expression. The more you do your soul work, the higher you will expand into new dimensions of sharing with the larger world. This is the key because the more you can be centered within yourself, the more you are able to achieve. It's time to let go of what we "think" we are meant to achieve and commit to the soul and allow it to unfold from there.

It just so happens that much of the system that we live in today has been shaped for us to follow a certain path. Which is birth, primary school, high school, university, work, and death. This is a system that nearly every human being follows or aspires to follow. There has been no time or curriculum placed in this system to do the inner education so that our work can reflect the highest cause for us and the greater world, which would ultimately connect us to the greater universe.

Chapter 10

Reshaping the Now

Every human is born into a set of conditions and beliefs, which have been cultivated through the relationship with their parents, family, culture, religion, media, environment and so much more. Many of us were lucky to scrape through a somewhat "normal" upbringing. But I'd have to say the majority of us have many layers to peel. If we can understand that pretty much every human being on the planet is going through the same process right now, it doesn't make us feel so alone! It's a collective shedding and once one individual takes the lead, many will follow. As a result, we become an inspiration to those around us and for the change that's possible all around the world.

If we can peel every layer of conditioning and programming away, we would realize that everyone is just like us! Without the belief of who we are – then who are we? That's a really interesting question to answer. Who are we without belief?

Once we have been stumped by this question, we begin to realize that identity is just a belief. Therefore, we can swap and change whenever we like; thus participating in multi-dimensions of knowledge and experience. The beauty in this is that the more experiences a person has in their life, the more opportunity they're given to grow and evolve. So what could be more valuable than being open to experience a vast range of colors?

To me, there's only one thing that top's this vast experience of many identities. That is our direct experience to the oneness. The participation in letting go of the belief of our own identity is the first movement into allowing ourselves to witness the oneness in all things. It doesn't mean we don't play in various roles (such as daughter, mother, father, girlfriend, doctor, school teacher etc) it just means that we feel comfortable in switching from one role to the next whenever we wish! Once we are able to truly appreciate this beauty of all expressions, we have stepped closer to a deep surrender; no matter what it appears to be on the surface (in more extreme cases such as religion, culture, creed). In order to accept everyone around us, we must have a level of surrender to fully allow each expression to be just as it is, whether we "believe" it to be right or wrong!

An exercise that you can put into daily practice is what I call "mind watch". It's a simple technique where you listen to the thoughts that are jumping around in your head while interacting with someone that creates discomfort for you. Maybe it's a boss at work that gets on your nerves or a family member who seems to poke you the wrong way? Once you start watching the mind, you'll start to see that it's your mind creating the discomfort and you get to choose the thoughts you're having and thus, choose your experience as well. This may be hard for people to break through initially because they were bought up with a very strong belief – such as a racist opinion. They were told that opinion every day of their life from the people they looked up to, only to then land themselves in a job or situation where they are working with someone who represents "that race". Naturally, the first thing that is going to jump into their mind will be all their beliefs and everything they have been told about that race. You could say, without even speaking to the person, they are already seeing them through a false lens. This is the moment that you get to put this game of "mind watch" into action.

If you play this game enough, you'll start to realize that all your thoughts and feelings about people are often coming from this conditioned part of yourself and that if you start to change your beliefs around people, the people also begin to change! Try it, its magic!

Letting go of old realities

Believe it or not, changing our belief system about the "outside" world is easier than it sounds. We must first take full responsibility by admitting that everything in our outside world is created from our inside world. Once we can take responsibility of this obvious fact, then we are empowered to go deeper and really change our life and learn how these beliefs first came to be. Most of the time, they came from either something we were told, or how we interpreted an event in the past. This could range from how we see the opposite sex, what our relationships are like, the way we approach challenges, how we see ourselves, what we think of the state of the world, our community, or even the way we live our life and the foods we eat. All this can be overwhelming if we think of it all at once. The good thing is that we don't have to. When we decide to just focus on the moment, we realize that whatever we need to discover in our life is available in that moment. There's no need to get ahead of our selves. In time, all shall be revealed and it will rise to the surface to be seen, challenged, and then finally understood.

The way we see the world around us is a direct projection of how we see ourselves. Sometimes we may choose to think; no, that it's just them and I am in fact "perfect"- yet a lot of the time, it's just our shadow self not wanting to take full responsibility. The best way I can tell if I'm making an accurate judgment of a person's character is to ask myself, "Do I have a charge around this person or the projection I'm seeing and if the answer is yes, then usually it is my own ego projecting?" If there is no charge but rather a greater level of compassion for the person, even if they are acting out of order, you are able to see that it's an accurate observation As we remove all the layers of the onion, we become more compassionate to the world around us. We are able to be more patient when others are out of line and more forgiving of those who have not yet broken free from the distractions and the illusions they are living in.

Many of the stories that have created our concept of reality have led us to living out habits that are less than supportive to our way of life. Much of the time, we make excuses for these habits. But if we want to be truly authentic with ourselves, then we will not shy away in excuses. Instead, we will stand strong by looking at our poor habits to find the blind spot in our thought pattern that's creating this behavior.

The main intention that every individual on the planet is striving for, whether they know it or not, is to be in a state of health and oneness. The reason is that being healthy is the most effortless state to be in. Due to many of the programs that have effected and shaped human consciousness, much of the world is out of balance with health today. As a result living less than graceful, effortless lives. Different priorities are now being put before health, such as money, work, quick pleasures, and mindless games.

How did we get to this current state of consciousness where the majority of the world's health is suffering on all levels from body, mind, and spirit? The answer lies within our belief in the stories we have been told and our lack of attention to resolving the pains and fears set in by these stories. What then makes it worse is that individuals are so petrified by the stories they are telling themselves everyday that they then make up excuses to protect their stories and the poor habits that come from these stories.

Let's take an obvious example of smoking cigarettes. We all know that smoking cigarettes is bad for your health. It's estimated that cigarette smoking accounts for 443,000 deaths each year in the United States. Plus it increases your chances of coronary heart disease, stroke, lung cancer, and various other diseases. The facts are there. Everyone who smokes cigarettes surely reads on the back of the pack what kind of trouble they could be getting into. It's blatantly obvious, since cigarette companies are now made to print on the back of the packet the threat of smoking. Yet people continue to do it! Why?

It's because of what I was referring to earlier on in this section. They are smoking cigarettes because of an unconscious program that tells them they need it. Maybe it helps them deal with "stress" or it brings them a state of calm. Yet what if our natural state is already a state of calm and relaxation and all they are really trying to relax are the many programs and thought forms that take them out of their natural state of calm. Surely it's more beneficial to simply remove the programs that take you away from your natural state rather than adding more layers to the onion and thus creating more disease and health challenges in the future.

One of the main problems in today's world is peoples inability to clear these programs. Instead, they stack more layers on their onion. Let's look at someone who's addicted to heroin. In this story, the individual first developed the addiction at a young age. Maybe they were not given the proper education about its ill health effects and they tried it just once. In the act it took them out of the pain they were feeling in their life, creating a feeling of peace and euphoria away from any issues. The experience was so good to them (since they no longer had to deal with their fears or programs) that they decided to return to the drug again and again. After a while, the drug starts to take such a hold on the individual until they're not only physically dependent on it, they're now so immune to the drug that they need higher and higher doses to get the same euphoric state. Years pass by and the veins in their arms have become so hardened that they can't even get a needle in there anymore and now they are searching for a way to feel comfort from the pain that continues to bubble up. By this stage, the individual may start to seek support in a "reputable" physician, who prescribes him something to get off heroin, only to addict him to another substance such as methadone or subtext – which are both far more addictive than heroin itself. The result is more layers of complexity in the individual.

Our society has been built in many strange ways and when we start to look beneath the surface of what is projected to be "good", we start to see the many layers of discord that are actually occurring. In ancient times, an individual would pay their doctor to keep them healthy. In today's world, it feels like we're paying our doctor to keep us sick. It's quite unnerving. So this individual, who has a deep history with addiction, fails in relieving the addiction through releasing the programs that are creating it. Instead, he is now trying everything he can to bury it deeper and deeper. As sad as this story is, it's what is occurring all around the world every day, not just with drug addicts, but also with regular people! The truth remains the same for whoever you are and until the program is released, the addiction will not go away.

Allowing new realities

Every moment that you are breathing gives you an opportunity to transform your reality. All you need are the right tools and understanding. Here are a few things to get you started.

You are not your thoughts. Thoughts are transient. They come and they go. One moment, you might be experiencing happy thoughts and the next moment sad and depressing thoughts. But the truth is none of these thoughts are your real identity. If they were, then every individual would be labeled as a schizophrenic, because how can your identity be two total opposites in one day or even in one minute.

You are the awareness. When you start to be watchful of the thousand thoughts that race around your head in one day, ask yourself who's watching these thoughts? This will lead you to your true identity because it's the part of you that never changes. It's the observer. Personalities and images will come and go but the observer will always stay the same.

You have the power of choice. From this space of awareness, you now have the power to choose how you wish to experience the game of life. This starts with how you want to perceive people, situations, and events. Through this power of choice, you can transform any situation into a positive one that helps you grow, evolve, and love. The reason why this becomes easy is because anything that rises to the surface gives you the ability to see it as an illusion, therefore the power to choose your reaction and feeling toward it.

There are many tools that allow us as individuals to transform our reality. But the question is, with so many realities available for experience, what is the best one for us? You may see thousands of motivational speakers, salesmen, and therapists, who are telling you, how to live, how to be, and how to see your life. But without actual contact to your true authentic self, you may become programmed once again by another belief system. Perhaps your new belief about yourself is happier, livelier, and more enthusiastic? This is a wonderful thing, yet without this one special ingredient (which I am about to describe) you may still feel like you are missing something, or even as though you have to prove yourself to the world in your new refurbished identity.

The special ingredient that I'm referring to requires no proof. It's so comfortable within itself that it simply allows all to be. You could have someone ridicule a person carrying this special gift but they will not find offence because they know themselves so well. This special ingredient I'm referring to is the oneness – the energy that connects all of creation and is not identified by any particular persona yet rather sees itself in everything, in perfect order.

Once an individual embodies this quality, the rainbow of expressions and gifts are able to shine forth uninhibited. The person becomes an open vessel to give anything a try. The reason they feel so free to give anything a go is because if they "fail", there's going to be no bruising of ego or damaging of identity: For there is nothing to protect and nothing to prove.

Can you imagine your life if you had nothing to protect and nothing to prove? There would be an automatic sense of liberation where your hearts dreams can come true. The reason why many people never pursue their life long dreams is because they're afraid that they might fail. Yet, without the ego of failure, all that remains is play!

The child is free

When we think back to our childhood, the majority of us could say that those younger years were the happiest times in our lives. As life continued to evolve, the magic and joy became lessened and life became more serious and stressful. But what if we could capture the energy of our youth and feel the magic that's available to us every day?

I guess the first step would be in understanding why we lose the continual inspiration for life in the first place? I have a few theories of what separates us from our continual joy and they are as follows:

As each year passes, we are being filled up with more and more programs from the media, our culture, the viewpoints of people around us, and our religions. Unless we have a dedicated meditation practice, we tend to get overwhelmed with too many thoughts. With all these opinions that run around in our head, it becomes difficult to know what our true nature is. All of these thoughts and opinions then start to affect our choices in life and before we know it, we are no longer running around outdoors with our child hood best friend, enjoying the vastness of our imagination. Instead, we are now cooped up in an office, calculating numbers and counting down the days until the weekend.

The second ingredient that I believe separates us from the pure enjoyment of every moment (and this one took me a long time to discover in my own life) is the addiction to achieving goals. I have always been a very ambitious person. After spending some time in deep meditation, I realized something quite unique. I feel much of the world may not understand this, at least until you experience it yourself, but I am compelled to share: All of the joy, love, and bliss that you could ever hope for as the result of any goal is available for you right here, right now.

I believe it's healthy to set goals so that there's a path set for creativity to expand and be expressed. But I believe many people are setting goals for the wrong reason. As a result, life becomes too complicated. There are many factors that motivate people and I could spend hours going into each area of motivation, but to be brief, here are a few points to consider for your obsession with achieving goals.

Be the best. From a very young age, we are taught that in order to be loved, we have to be the best. You can see this in every system that affects a child as they are growing. Schools are even geared this way. You are awarded for being the fastest, the most intelligent, the most creative, and the most talented. If you are not the best, then you often get mocked by other kids, frowned upon by the teachers, and sometimes even punished by your parents. This type of bruising can make a child want to do whatever it takes to succeed: Even if that means stepping on someone else's toes. This type of mentality leads you into a life, where you find yourself working 80 hours a week just to be the best.

Man on a mission, to save the world. Another individual may be really motivated toward a goal for what they believe to be a more "valuable" reason other than just getting love from others. It may be to save the world! But in their life-long mission to save the world, they forget to look after themselves or even the people around them. I've seen it a million times, especially in the human potentiality field, which is aimed to lift humanity up to new levels of personal power. I've seen producers of amazing events crumble underneath the pressure and instead of embodying what they are preaching to the world; they often become sleep deprived from too much work. Their health begins to suffer and the production team starts to argue because mistakes are made and there is a general stress that lives beneath the surface. On the surface however, everything appears to be smooth sailing. Yet, the people who are producing the event are falling apart.

Addiction to adrenalin

I have had friends who lived in New York City, the busiest business center of the world. These people have seen firsthand what the energy of the city does to you. Living in Los Angeles also had a similar affect on me. Yet, you do not realize it's affecting you in such a way because the fast pace can be addictive. This is due to the stress and pace causes your body to pump out adrenalin. I usually realize how much city energy affects me by day number three upon leaving the city. This is how the story plays itself out. I spend a good deal of time in the city. During this time, the movement of energy fuels me, moving me from meeting to meeting, driving through traffic, and finishing up errands on every corner of town. By the time the day is over, I am usually ready to pass out and get up and do it all over again.

Luckily for me, I've been able to spend a lot of time out of the city, surrounded by nature and the natural intelligence of the environment. When I first arrive at my destination, it usually takes me approximately three days to settle in. Believe it or not, at first, I feel quite uncomfortable settling into such a slow pace. My mind feels like it needs fuel and my body feels bothered. Normally, this then leads to a really long sleep of about 12 hours, followed by a couple days of decompressing and then out of nowhere, an energy arises inside of me that I had forgotten about while being in the city. It's a stillness that is in tune with nature – an awareness that is connected to the silence.

I hope this story illustrates how your location has an effect on your ability to connect to the freedom of the child within you. We must not mistake our addiction to adrenalin verses our natural state of silence. Once I'm in touch with this silence (which is really your connection to the oneness) the inspiration for creativity and expression begin to pour out and I find myself feeling the joy of my inner child once again. Now that we understand what can divert us, let's see what can assist us to embody our inner child.

Becoming the inner child

For those who do not yet understand the concept of the inner child, allow me to differentiate between being childish and being childlike. Childish is a quality that comes from someone of immaturity who doesn't want to take responsibility – one who lacks the ability to be present with those around them. Whereas childlike is a quality that comes out of that direct presence. It's a purity of the heart that loves everyone and everything and therefore, is able to access complete joy from its surroundings.

When a child is first born, any stranger can look into that child's eyes and will see a person that holds no judgment. The child is open, trusting, and available to share love. As the child becomes older, its ability to remain open depends on the conditionings it has been given. As its identity becomes more defined and structured, the child then has its own set of guidelines as to whom he can trust, how he sees the world, and who he allows himself to love and not love. Since we can understand this, we can then realize that the less we cast judgment on the world around us, the more we are available to experience that love.

Exercise to awaken your inner child

Here is a short exercise for you to find the qualities of your own inner child and how you can bring them into your life today. Describe the earliest memory you have of feeling free and happy?

What were the different emotions and feelings you had during this time?

What was it about that scene that made it so magical?

What stories or beliefs have you told yourself today? Only include those, which do not allow you to feel these positive feelings and emotions in every moment?

What feelings could you take from this memory that would allow you to feel more connected to the pure joy of life right now?

What steps are you going to take to implement this freedom and joy into your life every day?

Merging back into oneness

Through the search for harmony in our life, we often seek to move away from pain. The current human perception of moving away from pain is skewered into an awkward viewpoint. It sounds a little like this, "If I try to avoid the pain as much as I can, then it will be ok and it will go away". Yet, it's that exact viewpoint that creates more pain. In order to re-unite with our oneness to all things, we must peel off the layer that tells us to avoid pain. Rather, we should embrace pain with all of our heart. This will create a perfect state of harmony within our body, mind, and spirit.

In my time working as a yoga therapist in a drug and alcohol/detox treatment center in Mexico, I had the chance to work with guiding individuals back into a sate of balance through their body, mind, and spirit. While in the process of working with these patients, I was also able to gain a deeper understanding on what creates pain in the body, as well as the mind and emotions and I've come to realize that unless we fully embrace all of our pain, whether that be an emotional memory, or a discomfort in the body, or a physical addiction, we'll never be able to truly transform. This avoidance of feeling the pain is what often creates these addictive behaviors.

If we were to spend time studying with a Shaolin monk, we would see that many of these great masters from this tradition are able to endure incredible pain and punishment. What makes them so remarkable is they don't shy away from pain. They've gone through intense training with mental discipline and meditation that allows them to embrace the pain and move through it in a different way. I don't consider myself a martial artist, but wisdom does not require a label. If wisdom is accurate, then you can apply it to any religion, way of life, or technique and the answer will be the same. This is why I'm referring to martial arts in connection to dealing with emotional pain or any other type of pain.

I've seen amazing martial artists work with energy in a way that's beyond the current physical status quo. These individuals have trained their whole life to understand their connection to the larger quantum field and their unity with all things. Not just an intellectual understanding, but a practical understanding through the sacred arts. There are masters who can light paper on fire with the energy of their hands and individuals who can bend spoons and move objects with the power of their chi. to someone who's so conditioned by the belief systems of the world; they may say that's impossible! Those who cannot fathom such skills are the people who have bought into the belief that life in finite rather than infinite. In an infinite world, anything is possible and in a finite world, only the things that you have been taught are possible. Which one are you?

The beautiful thing is these ancient arts have been around for centuries and date back into ancient times. You can find them inscribed over Egypt's ancient pyramids or in the caves of Tibetan masters. Yet, countless civilizations have come and gone over the many thousands of years on this planet. With the movement from each civilization to the next, the story has slowly changed and much of the wisdom has been forgotten: Each new civilization then re-establishing itself in a different system of belief. Slowly over time, the ancient wisdom has been integrated out of society rather than into society. Perhaps the additional layers of illusion come from the new king's agenda to conquer more land? Maybe this king cares more about himself than his people, and decides to create a belief within his people that it is a noble quality to die for your country. So thousands of men sign up to kill, pillage, and rape without any respect for the people in neighboring territories. All of which came from the belief that stemmed from separation consciousness.

True wisdom is a space of oneness

True wisdom comes from a place that honors the unique connection of all things. This is our oneness. When we are able to embody this connection to all things, then a natural harmony starts to occur and we move into a synchronistic flow with the rest of creation. No longer do we need to struggle. Instead, we recognize and remember that we are a part of a greater whole and that we're all in it together. This state of consciousness automatically accepts its natural intelligence that is the order of micro-cosm and macro-cosm of the universe. This works the same way in which a flower will point its face to the sun in order to grow taller. The flower doesn't need to read a textbook on how to grow. It's simply in tune with the greater intelligence of itself (the micro) and the greater world around itself (the macro).

For example, the micro-cosm of the flower automatically knows what it needs to do in order to grow and sustain itself, such as building cells, and transforming sunlight into energy. This is part of the equation. While symbiotically the macro-cosm, which is its connection to the larger universe, becomes tuned into seeking sunlight, water, and nutrients from the soil around it. All of these aspects outside the flower are the flowers connection to the macro-cosm of the universe. Then we decide to introduce a new species, such as the bees, which also live in symbiosis with their greater intelligence of creation (a space of oneness). As the bee gathers nectar from a flower, tiny grains of pollen stick to its hairy legs and body. When the bee flies to another flower for nectar, the pollen on its legs and body brushes off to help fertilize the next flower. I'm positive that the bee didn't think about this process. Rather it is a natural occurrence created through the bee's intelligence within its own needs and thus bringing benefit to all the other flowers in the garden.

As you can see, it doesn't matter who you are. Whether you're a flower, an insect, or a human being, we can all benefit from tapping into this greater intelligence of oneness.

Gratitude promotes our connection to oneness

Just like the flowers, bees, and every other living being on the planet, as humans we have been blessed with the gift of life. And with this one gift alone, we have also been granted infinite potential to celebrate this life with various talents, skills, and passions. Also, we have family, friends, and an awesome planet with an array of spectacular environments, climates, and colorful scenery to choose from! We have been given this gift unconditionally. From the moment we are born, it is up to us to celebrate it. We can be appreciative of this gift or we can seek to find reasons why this gift was not such a great gift in the first place.

When we choose to look at this gift with a negative spin and lack appreciation, then we automatically move into a contracted state of consciousness. The world around us starts to collapse because our viewpoint is telling us that we are limited. When we choose to look at our life in appreciation, then the world around us starts to expand and we become more open to receive and celebrate greater depths and higher heights of this gift.

Due to the many layers and programs currently embedded in our society, an individual on the planet are often swinging between high highs and low lows. One minute they are over the moon, ecstatically excited by life and at other times, suicidal, depressed, or in deep anxiety. This rollercoaster ride has been given to us through the programs we picked up along the way, and our attachment to these programs. The current state of the modern world is more interested in material wealth than inner wealth, which means to say the wealth on the outside, rather than the inside.

People have been so misguided that they believe the outside representation of wealth is true happiness, forgetting that as you establish true inner health, the outside world will also reflect that same wealth. You cannot do it the other way around. You cannot force an image of wealth on the outside unless you develop it on the inside because if you are sad and depressed, no amount of luxury can change it unless you change it inside first.

The best stepping-stone to inner and outer wealth is the energy of gratitude. This one quality prepares the inner environment and the outer environment for abundant receiving and sharing. When an individual develops gratitude in their life, that gratitude begins to spread into all of their endeavors, relationships, personal activities, and inner contemplations – thus creating a greater feeling of oneness with all of creation.

Most of us have areas in our life where we are ecstatically thankful and other areas that may be a challenge. Maybe you have a lot of gratitude for your husband's cooking and how he always has a meal for you when you get home from work. At the same time, you might lack appreciation for your boss at work as he is always pressuring you to work overtime, thus forcing you to arrive home late from work to a cold dinner.

It is interesting how each aspect of our life is in constant play with every other aspect of our life. The trick is to choose to see the appreciation in it all. Just like the bee that pollinates the flower, every aspect of your life is dependent on the other aspects to live. For example, in order for your husband to cook a good meal for you when you get home from work, there must be money. In order to get money, you must have a job. In order to have a job, you must have qualifications or go to school. In order to get to school, you must have a car and so on. As you can see, this is the web of life. It's all connected and every aspect makes all the other aspects possible. So instead of just being appreciative for the home cooked meal, you may start to develop an appreciation for your job and your boss who pays you each week so that you can go grocery shopping.

When we start to see how every part of life is vitally dependent on every other aspect, a new quality of gratitude starts to develop and as more gratitude develops, more joy is delivered. As gratitude expands, so does your connection to the universe and without any effort, you begin experiencing a vast connection to the oneness.

Have you ever been in a conversation with a stranger and had an instant connection, as if you have known them for your whole life? Maybe you have the same interests or they see life in a similar way to you, making life feel easy when they're around? This is an experience of oneness. You are relating to them as if they were your mirror as you agree with them and appreciate their viewpoint.

This experience of oneness may be available to you with specific friendships, yet not all of them. You may have a really effortless connection with some people while others require a little more work. Those people in your life that require more work are often labeled in your mind in a way that either judges them or puts them in a category of difficult. And most the time the belief is "They are difficult", rather than recognizing there is something inside of you resisting them. So next time instead of judging them, find what you are grateful for, and perhaps you will start experiencing more oneness.

Oneness takes no effort

Take a moment now to think of a relationship in your life that requires a little more effort than the rest. Maybe it is a family member, a boss, or someone who you constantly pushes your buttons. Now that you have found that person, think back to a time when you experienced turbulence with them. In reflecting on this experience, take note of what types of thoughts were running through your head. Maybe you were offended or affected by them in a way that made you feel uncomfortable? Notice how the thoughts and opinions are making you feel. Perhaps your thoughts and opinions of this person's behavior are valid? Now ask yourself, "Who are your opinions valid to?" If you look deep enough, you'll see that the opinion is only valid to the identity that it's offending and if you carry a different identity, it may not offend you at all.

Let's look at an example. A vegetarian may be completely repulsed by someone who's eating meat. At the same time, another meat eater would not be offended at all because the two meat eaters feels a sense of oneness together, because they like the same food. On the other hand, the vegetarian may be offended by the behavior of the meat eater and end up in a fight.

Now being a vegetarian myself I could say yes, the vegetarian has an intelligent and more holistic viewpoint for their diet. Yet, this scenario presents a double-edged sword. That's because they might feel oneness with the animals and they love preaching about loving animals, yet they are unable to preach love for the person they are judging. So on one side of the coin, the person is feeling immense oneness with the animals while on the other side, a real lack of connection with the person who eats meat.

We are all doing the best we can when it comes to our love and compassion for the world around us. At times, it's hard to stay connected to that oneness when we feel that there's an injustice-taking place. That injustice could be toward our self, to a certain race, our country, or even to our favorite football team. The truth is whoever or whatever we decide to put value on, this area will be a tender spot for us if it's damaged. But in truth, if we are to speak from a very high level, every individual that we have ever hated or had conflict with is a reflection of ourselves and we are really having conflict with our self. We may not realize it at the time, but the reason why we are experiencing conflict in certain aspects of our life, or people in our life, is because there's something in that situation that brings us fear. So in order to "control" the fear we try to "control" the situation rather than feeling the fear or pain as mentioned previously and moving through it. Once we are able to see that our own fears and pains create the conflict (and not the other way around) then we give ourselves the opportunity to move through it. Unless we can take responsibility for our own feelings, we will never get over the conflict. The person may change or the situation may look different, but you'll start to see a pattern of the same conflict appearing over and over again. The conflict is in you and not in them.

As soon as we shift our own inner conflict, the people around us, and the situations start to change. I remember working as a host at a restaurant many years ago. Every single waiter and employee at the restaurant had an issue with the boss. Rightfully so, since he would rip off almost everyone's tips and make them work strenuous hours without breaks, while hitting on the women and making provocative comments. Everyone at the restaurant had an opinion and guess who got to hear all the opinions – me! Working at the front desk, I would get everyone's judgment and viewpoint. What I noticed was the individuals at the restaurant who were a little tougher on their exterior would had the most gripes to report about the boss and those individuals who had less inner issues would have less gripe to share.

The individuals with the most gripes would come up to me complaining about everything under the sun. I would sit there and listen, without comment or judgment. As I sat back to witness all of this revealing itself to me, I decided to make it my mission to become best friends with the boss and to see the good in this person regardless of the appearances. I could have easily dropped into the same judgment as everyone else; sure he made the odd suggestive comment to me and would look at me in ways that proposed his interest. But instead of being affected by it, I decided to simply hold my own balance by standing in integrity with myself, and showing him love and compassion. I didn't feel threatened because I began to see that inside this big boy bully suit, he was really just a young child with unresolved issues like the rest of the world. As I began to show him care and compassion for the events taking place in his life, he began to open up to me. The sly and provocative comments began to stop. I became a trusted ally and instead of an awkward work situation, I began to get perks that no one else was having, without trading any part of my dignity and self worth.

This story illustrates how we have the power to change any situation to something of greater oneness if only we choose to see through a lens of love and compassion. These two qualities alone are the greatest force when it comes to moving back into a space of oneness.

Chapter 11

Choosing your Mastery

What is mastery?

Every individual on the planet are on the same path of mastery, but how we get there may be a totally different path. However in truth, the underlining qualities of any master are the same. A master has truly moved into a space of knowing their interconnection to all things. They are able to step outside the perceived identities of the ego that seek a selfish pleasure and recognize a greater pleasure, which is that of the whole in equal benefit and balance.

Many mothers are a wonderful example of mastery when it comes to taking care of their children. They have stepped outside of their selfish needs and find pleasure in the child's happiness and comfort. It's as if their child's pleasure is their own pleasure. This is an example of someone stepping into a greater space of heart energy, intuition, and care. This is the same for a master who has moved into a place of oneness with the greater universe. Everyone around them is like that child and receives the same level of intuitive love to the next person. A master does not discriminate. Yet, they are able to operate from a larger space of awareness that instantly knows the best way to act in any given situation. A master, who is truly developed, does not require much "thinking" but rather, there intuitive guidance moves them in a perfected way. This is just like the bee that flies from each flower to get nectar and in the same process pollinating every flower. This is all part of the bees pure intelligence, because it's in tune with the greater oneness, therefore everything benefits.

Colors in the rainbow

Every person on the planet is expressed as a different color in the rainbow. As we embody our purest color and frequency, we can create the brightest rainbow on the rainiest day!

The beautiful thing about being human is that we get to choose what gifts we wish to express. These gifts may range from physical talents such as riding a surfboard, to creating pottery with our hands, to mental talents such as developing an equation to describe the theory of relativity. The list goes on and on. There's no end to the list of talents that are available for each person on the planet. What makes this even more remarkable is that not everyone is drawn to the same gifts. Some people prefer to ponder what created the universe, while others are more interested in experiencing the universe by riding a wave at their local beach. Wherever you are and however you're being called to pursue your talents and interests is perfect for you and your unique expression. We may not realize it, but everything that we do is giving us direct feedback to how the greater universe operates.

In today's world, more and more athletes and highly successful business people are learning that having a meditation practice can be highly beneficial to the success of your career. Why? Because when the mind has been cleared of the many layers of confusion, drama, and emotional unrest, it can operate better. Meditation works in a way that clears the mind of all these thought patterns, thus giving the person a greater feeling of peace and clarity. Once this has been achieved, the individual is able to better focus on the task at hand and the results they wish to achieve.

Meditation has many benefits. Not only does it allow you to create more peace and harmony in your life, it also connects you to oneness. When a person first starts to meditate, they may feel as though they can't stop their mind from racing a mile a minute – from one thought to the next. It can be very frustrating to someone who believes that meditation is meant to be peaceful. In fact, in the beginning stages of meditation, one might find that the act of meditation itself is anything but peaceful. Still, directly after the practice they feel more peace. Why? Because they have just spent the last 20 minutes allowing the energy that was so suppressed beneath the surface, to rise and be released. The trick is to always return your mind back to a state of meditation.

A simple meditation practice

Sit up-right or against a wall so that your back is straight, close your eyes, and listen for the in and out breath coming from your nose. Keep your awareness on this process and every time your mind starts to wonder, simply bring your mind back to the in and out breath. Feel the pace of the breath, the flow, the movement, and keep your attention there.

Even the greatest of meditation experts sometimes find trouble keeping their mind focused, especially if it's a time when they are experiencing challenges in life. But if you commit to doing meditation for at least 20 minutes a day, you will start to notice that your pressures are no longer pressures. You begin to move into more of an effortless flow and those challenges simply disappear.

As we start to master the mind and return to a space of quiet stillness, we start to get insight into areas of our life that require assistance. In meditation, it is a natural occurrence for individuals to receive direct clarity on how to solve a problem. I've experienced this countless number of times. The beauty in this is that while meditating, we don't look for answers because this starts the mind thinking and then the thinking mind, which only knows the stories of the past, can only give you a limited answer. Instead, by relinquishing all need to find an answer or solution and instead focusing on the meditation, the natural harmony, and your experience with oneness, delivers you an answer that is beyond the thinking of the regular mind. It is quite miraculous.

The deeper we go into stillness, the more profound our understanding of our self, and the world around us appears. It's quite remarkable. The reason I say this is because the greater the stillness, the less we are identified with our own self-created drama. Thus, we have more resources to tune into the larger universe and intelligence.

In today's world, we may often hear people comment, "Oh, that person is a master at that sport or that skill." and the fact is, they are very talented. What I'm proposing is a different level of mastery. Not just the type of mastery that comes with a highly skilled individual, but someone who posses the qualities of true wisdom and understanding. This requires a different type of training – meditation being one of them, along with the everyday practice of seeing yourself in the mirror wherever you go –in the people that you love and the people that cause you difficulty. If we are able to see ourselves everywhere, then we are able to develop qualities such as compassion, tolerance, acceptance, forgiveness, and love which I believe are some of the richest qualities of an individual who embodies oneness.

With this fast paced society, we often get so swept away with the movement that we forget to stop, breath deep, and witness the eternal energy inside of us. Our lack of presence is sometimes created by all of the goals that have been set partly by our ego. Believe me, your ego will be the last one to admit that your goals are controlled by ego. Maybe you're running a program that believes in order to be happy, you must achieve this goal. As a result you end up spending every waking minute trying to achieve it. This program keeps you moving toward your goal, thinking that your mastery is in the distant future. The truth is that your mastery is right here, right now. If we can remember this one fact in every moment, we will never be separated from our mastery.

The reason I say this is because when we are totally unified to this present moment, then we have all of our resources and energy available to make this moment the best moment to ever exist. If we are thinking about the future while in this moment, then we will have missed the moment all together. There have been many amazing people who have lived on this planet; some of those people have achieved extraordinary feats in their career, changing the course of the story on planet Earth. Some of those people sacrificed their health in order to achieve their goals while others achieved their goals while remaining in good health. Which one will you be?

Refining your tools as a master

Everyone, no matter who you are, is offered a path for transformation. Some people take longer to realize this beautiful truth, which simply means they take the slightly longer road to understanding the wisdom of their wholeness. But sooner or later, they will realize it. Full-embodied oneness doesn't just happen all of a sudden, (unless of course you are a Sadhu meditating in cave for your whole life) for most of us; it is a process of growth. Every step of the way, we are calculating and understanding. Sometimes we may feel lost, but really this just means we have more material to work through in order to get the right answers. As mentioned before, this is why practicing meditation is a great tool. In addition to meditation and other spiritual practices, I have 5 points of reference, which you can ask yourself in order to track your mastery. They are as follows.

5 steps to mastery

My own insecurities verse the greater whole?

Many of us live our life, trying to prove to everyone else around us how good we are. Perhaps this comes from a lack of self-esteem created by a program earlier on in life or perhaps you believe your parents or friends will look down on you if you were not successful. Whatever created your insecurity is the same ingredient that is blocking you from experiencing oneness. Did you ever notice that when there is less pressure you feel more comfortable being yourself? When we are carrying out a task simply for the joy of expressing, then we're giving all of our energy back to creation and this is the greatest gift ever. On the other hand, if you are working in an orphanage helping sick children, only because it is a "good cause" but are not really enjoying it, then you are running low on resources. Every person is responsible for them self and if we can find our own inner joy, then whatever pursuit we are inspired to do, we will feel at ease with our life.

Some people may think that I'm contradicting myself. One minute, I'm saying that true oneness brings a greater level of love and compassion to the wider world around you, and the next, I'm saying you must care about your happiness first before others. This is why I'm trying to illustrate that it's not one or the other. In fact, when we bring true happiness inside, it automatically overflows into the outside world at the same time. However if we are seeking happiness for our ego, then it will never be enough to overflow. Instead, we will keep on taking and taking from the outside world, never sharing our energy in return.

Be patient, we have eternity

In todays fast pace world, patience seems to be one of the hardest qualities to find. People want everything now, and as a result, life has become out of balance. The biggest illusion that I believe the world has bought into is that we must hurry because we are running out of the time. This belief in this program is what created our problems in the first place. When we believe that we are running out of time, then we start to rush, skip steps, cut corners, and find any way to reach our destination before it's too late. In the process of doing this, we are actually creating more difficulty for ourselves, and the world around us. This belief system has played itself into every part of the modern world, from prescription medicines that offer a quick fix by numbing the pain, to how we behave in personal relationships, such as needing to have an answer now, rather than peacefully giving each other time to think and realize the wisdom that needs to be found in time.

We are currently living in a world that is running on a treadmill, forgetting that the most intelligent wisdom is 'taking our time'. The sun, which is one of our planets most impressive gifts, does not wake up one day and say to itself, "Man I better hurry with this day because I have to get to the other side of the planet before its too late. If I don't, then half the planet may die!" No, the sun simply follows its path without haste, serving the whole planet, all its people, plants, and environment exactly what they need to survive.

With the current "threat" of global warming and the pressing challenges our Earth is going through, I believe instead of racing the clock, we slow down the clock. It's only our addiction to our perceived needs that make us move so fast in the first place. If every individual on the planet agreed to do less and enjoy nature a little more, I could see a whole new way of living develop on the planet. For starters, we would be driving our cars less, and perhaps eating more vegetables, nuts, seeds, and fruits, thus allowing the whole meat industry to rest, which contributes to more of the CO_2 emissions than car fuel itself. We would be on our way to balancing out the problems that many people say are growing. On top of that, if we took more time to relax, we may start to realize that these truly are the most fulfilling things available to us on the planet.

Too many of us get swept away by big careers, big cars, and big houses, without any substance to fill them with. I've traveled to some of the most challenging places on the planet, where famine and disease are high. Yet, some of these places carry with them a fullness of heart that you sometimes don't experience in the fast paced consumer driven society.

I'm not suggesting that everyone heads out and buy a cardboard box and set up real estate on his or her local railroad track. What I am suggesting is that these people had created a sense of community, which was local to their small area on the planet and they not only knew who their neighbors were, they were actively supporting each other in creating life. It wasn't about who has the biggest house. It had become a necessity that they help each other out, because one day, they may need the same assistance.

Connecting to our local community plays a big part in slowing down the pace of life. I'm sure that there are many people who were once so swept away with life that they didn't have time for their family. It wasn't until a family member passed away that they wished they had more time together. All of this for the price of what? Extra money in the bank? Another car to drive? Or more fame and success?

What part of me is creating this story?

Many of us go through times in our life when we don't feel completely comfortable. Maybe we are in a relationship that has turned sour or we are facing a challenge at work. This may be hard to realize, but everything you are experiencing is a direct result of the thoughts and opinions you are carrying around in your subconscious. Since our subconscious is usually the part that hides from our full awareness, it's understandable that at times we may not be able to take responsibility for it. So next time you feel a challenge, ask yourself the following question: What part of myself is unable to move into full acceptance right now?

The moment we are able to move into full acceptance is the moment we are able to let it go. Maybe you are fighting with your husband or wife for a few days and you have been through a screaming match and now the energy is just a little awkward in the air. You have moved past the intensity and now you just feel awkward. Maybe you would even like to create a little peace and just move on, but this awkward feeling is lingering and you don't know what to do. In this example, what you are feeling is the pressure that the other individual is still holding in their mind, along with your uncertainty of how to act. Most people would say to make a mends, do your best at winning the other person over. However, unless the other individual is prepared to release his or her own tension, there's nothing you can do to help. You are only responsible for your own story and what you are telling yourself. So rather than trying to fix it from the outside, which may or may not work, you should change the story from the inside.

Changing the story from the inside means being loving to yourself and recognizing that you are not responsible for everyone's feelings around you. You are only responsible for your own peace. You can't change someone's state of being. That is up to them. This step is great because it allows you to move away from a feeling of powerlessness and into a feeling of your own power. The next step is to forgive and let go of any area within that needs something from the other individual to feel better. Maybe you feel that if they apologized, you could get over it. Not until they apologize will you fully move on. This thought and belief could leave you stuck in a feeling of anxiety and grief your whole life because you can't make them apologize or even make them feel remorse for you. So we must let go of needing that from the other person. So to refresh:

You are responsible for your own feelings and no one else's. No one else is responsible for your feelings. By applying these two methods, you are automatically taken out of this weaving. Anything that they say to you or don't say to you can't trigger any feelings of uncomfortably now. Here is a short exercise. If you are in a conflict with someone the following exercise will assist you to clear yourself from any uncomfortable feelings.

Creating your own story
Describe the situation and why it makes you feel uncomfortable:

What areas do you wish you could change in this situation?

What areas for do you want to change within them (such as changing the way they feel) that you are not responsible for?

What areas within yourself can you change that will make you feel more comfortable in this situation?

How can you love yourself more, and what positive affirmations can you tell yourself to make you feel comfortable?

Transform and inform with gratitude
A master is someone who remains connected to the expansive field of oneness even in the toughest of circumstances. This awareness of oneness automatically puts us in a state of gratitude because we are recognizing how powerful and profound creation is and our place in creation. With all the stars, planets, and grains of sand in our galaxy alone, one can look on this, startled in

amazement and awe for being intricately connected to it all and a part of its continual flow. The excellence that has come together to create the Earth which we live on and its faultless distance from the sun, creating the perfect temperature and ecology for us to live in, breath in, and thrive in and that is just us and our planet! This amazing balance that has created our life is one of the many reasons why each and every day we should wake up in gratitude. Most of the time, we get so lost in the smaller details that we forget to open our hearts in gratitude for every moment. If we were able to see how profound each and every moment is, then just like a child, we would transmute the smaller details into the pure wonder and magic that they truly are.

An adult is someone who has forgotten that they are still a child at heart. It's up to us to invite that inner child back into our life whenever we can because it's our inner child that connects to this feeling of oneness and gratitude. You may say to yourself, "I'm not a child." My response to this is that there is a difference between being a child and behaving immaturely versus letting your inner child out to play. Your inner child is the free flowing love that seeks only to connect with the people and the environment around them. When your inner child connects to the other inner child of a business associate, a deeper connection develops. This connection is shared oneness. No longer is it the mind, the intelligence, or the personas relating to each other – it's now the wonder, enchantment, and the love of life connecting together and harmonizing. This doesn't mean that you cannot sell a billion dollar deal at the table. It simply means that through connecting on this level, you are actually creating a deeper love and connection. An innate trust actually supports any business deal you may be venturing into. After all, I'm sure you would feel more comfortable doing business with someone who you feel a deeper connection with, rather than someone who is just good on paper.

How do you step away from the meeting of the minds and into a meeting of the hearts? For any given situation, ask yourself this one question, "What am I grateful for right now?" Then start looking for all the reasons why you are grateful with this person. At first, it may be hard. But after a while, you will start to realize that there are infinite reasons to be grateful. This will then start to shift your consciousness to your true expanded state and while doing it, the way you see your relationship with this person will surely change. You will soon find that as you give others gratitude, they naturally want to return it – and so the cycle continues. It's a really fun game to play!

Simple acceptance creates transformation

There may be areas in your life that just seem to be unchangeable at times. Maybe you have tried everything to get a different result and regardless of the effort, nothing seems to work. This is the moment we get to put pure acceptance into practice! This is sometimes the hardest thing for us to apply, especially when we are so attached to having a specific outcome. But the irony in that much like a lot of my thoughts, by moving into pure acceptance, you are actually creating space for your intention to exist.

I've had a friend who shared a story with me about his father, who was a raging alcoholic. No matter what their family said or did, they couldn't convince their father to stop drinking. They would try everything, but he would not stop. In fact, the more pressure they put on him, the more he would drink. One day my friend mentioned to me that he had come to a new realization and that was: just because his father was unhealthy, it didn't mean that he had to become unhealthy worrying about him. So he started to back off and give his father some space. My friend stopped making side comments to his father about his issues and started to just enjoy their time together. The rest of the family began to adopt the same level of acceptance and collectively chose to love their father no matter how he chose to live his life. This level of acceptance was the alchemy that transformed their father into a success story and later, their father mentioned that as soon as the pressure was off, he felt like he could make his own decisions, clearly look at his life, and make a choice that felt right to him. His drinking has now come down to a minimum and he is healthier than ever.

This story is but one illustration of how moving into pure acceptance can assist you in actually manifesting your intentions.

Another example of moving into acceptance to assist greater balance is in relieving painful memories. When you are attempting to process a painful memory and you cannot come close to forgiving the person involved, life can become a struggle. Perhaps you are dealing with a trauma that was really damaging such as molestation or rape. These types of experiences are some of the most traumatic wounds to heal and many people spend their whole life in bitter resentment for the pain created from these experiences. The truth is that you are only causing yourself more pain and disease by hanging on in resentment. The pain and anger builds up in the body, creating further disconnection in your surrounding relationships, in addition furthering dis-ease and sickness in the body. It is a commonly known fact that unprocessed emotions create cell degeneration, thus a shutting down of the body's vital life force. Given this reality, we must seek to find a way of returning to harmony. Sometimes forgiveness or loving the person that committed the act is just too far out of reach to do earlier on in the game. This is why the best place to begin is acceptance. By accepting, you are not saying that the other person's actions were right. Instead, you are simply accepting that it happened. You are acknowledging the reality of it. In the act of acknowledging and accepting, you are empowering yourself to no longer hold onto old emotions that only build up in your system and cause more pain.

Acceptance can sometimes even be a hard place to reach if you have been in strong denial. Conceivably, it may be too painful to look at. Yet, the moment we are able to stare pain in the face is the moment that it goes away. You may have a close friend or councilor who can support you in looking at the pain and accept what has happened. You certainly cannot change the fact that it happened. So the best thing you can do is to love yourself enough to look deeper and acknowledge the happening. This is by far the greatest gift you can give yourself because soon enough, you will find peace again. You deserve that.

Beyond the Mortal Story

It is our stories and beliefs that continue to drive us towards our needs and wants in life. Many of our basic needs are important for the maintenance of this temple we live in (our bodies) and the vitality of our days. Yet, I would have to say the majority of our needs and wants are perpetuated by the stories. If we were to turn our attention to the great masters from any religion, we would see that there needs had risen above the mortal stories that often create addiction and drama. They have surrendered their life to something greater than them. They may call their God by a different name, but they have all participated in the same act – surrendering their life to a higher power.

Chapter 12

A New World Begins with You

There is so much more available to us in every moment than we can see with the physical eye. The depth and love that the universe holds us in is like a child to its mother's bosom. We are supplied for, because we are gracefully woven into the divine plan. In truth, we have never left the bosom of the creative life force that first birthed us into existence because we are that life force and it is us. There is no separation. We have just spent time forgetting. But now we are ready to remember.

We have spent lifetime upon lifetime in denial of our true nature, buying into the stories and programs that tell us we are anything but whole and complete. Yet the truth is, we are complete and far more connected to the eternity of the universe than our intelligent minds can calculate. The poet was born from a place of intimate connection to this field of mystery. We are all poets, expressing with curious eyes the wonders and charms of our infinite self in all its expressions and forms. Yet, along the way we became so hypnotized by these infinite expressions and became lost and forgot our true source and supply of perfect intelligence – the intelligence of oneness.

There is no right or wrong. It is all a part of the whole and one side of the coin will always have another side to balance its face. As humanity, we have played every story fathomable to our creative genius inside. We have build monuments, grand structures, and civilizations and have watched them crumble all beneath our own power. The games have been extraordinary. We have been glorified in the heights of joy and success and broken down in the distress of pain and loss. We have chosen it all, every last millisecond has been chosen by us, for the pure experience of knowing what it feels like.

There has come a time now, one that will stand out in human history. Much like many of the great revolutions, this will play precedent to them all. It is the great awakening, the remembering, and the time to dream awake.

A time to give thanks

There comes a time in our lives when we say to ourselves enough is enough. Maybe you have been in an abusive relationship for the past ten years and one day, it dawns on you, and enough is enough. I am ready to move on from this story and to create a beautiful life – the life I was truly designed for. This type of story of realization is happening all over the planet right now and is available for you to. What areas of your life have you been dealing with, because you have been to shy to stand up for your real worth or for demanding a life of grace, joy, and harmony? Any place of doubt that has ever lived inside of your soul is now ready to be released and you are ready to fly free, to spread your wings and leave all those old stories behind.

You should not fear this step, for all of humanity is doing it with you. We are doing it together and as one person opens their wings, we immediately give everyone else an opportunity to do the same. So what are you waiting for? Spread your wings and fly and know that as the great masters who showed the way; don't look back, instead lead the way. That's what you are asked to do.

As your story changes, the whole world's story will change to. For centuries we have bowed our heads to religious figures – statues that would promise us a better life and attended pilgrimages with the intention to have a blessed life; when all along it was us creating a good or bad life. It was our own beliefs and our own perceptions that delivered us our prayers. One day, God was cruel and the next day God was nice. Yet it was our own label that distorted God and how we viewed our perception of this creative force. We gave our power away, thinking that our destiny was in the hands of something or someone outside ourselves. As a result, we lived stories that were less than beautiful. We put up with mediocre living, painful diseases, broken relationships, and hatred in our hearts. All because of our disconnection to the true God, the one that lives inside of us all, that is no better than anyone or anything, yet is rather perfect oneness with all things.

Today each and every one of us are invited to bow our heads to our own heart – to honor the divine qualities of self and to bow our head to love ourselves. The moment we stop bowing our head to the God outside of ourselves is the moment we truly recognize the god is within ourselves, and that God is within each and every person on the planet. This action is not an opportunity for the ego to think that it is better than the outside world. Rather, it is an action for the divinity of love to rise in every human being so that we can recognize our oneness in the grand plan of this intelligent cosmos. That way we can see ourselves pulsing with creation, moving in a synchronized flow, in the same way that the moon pulls the tides and the bees create the honey and the flowers point there face to the sun. All of creation pulsating in one heart beat, breathing with one breath, and loving with one heart. This is not some fantasy or a dream of some distant goal. This is already happening. We are already moving in this pulse. We are already one with creation. You can decide to remember now or continue on living in an illusion that is always seeking to find its home.

You can choose to find your connection to oneness now, or later. It is up to you. There is no right or wrong. Every individual's choice to remember or forget is up to them. Some people have been through enough pain that they don't want to forget anymore. They want to remember their perfect connection to everything – their true state of existence which is the balance and harmony of the whole universe, moving together in a continual flow.

The only way out of this game is to remember. The way of remembering is to release the stories that keep you in separation and judgment. Take this moment to remember and forgive all the stories that have ever let you down and recognize their perfection in leading you home to this moment right now. Everything was created for you. To lead you to this exact place right now – to this moment of remembering – so that you may appreciate it all.

The depth of appreciation

Have you ever heard the saying, "You don't know what you've got until it's gone." Think of your journey through time as a process of forgetting so that when you remember again, you would have more appreciation for it.

A young child living in Africa, who has never experienced a warm bed at night, only knows life on the streets, battling for food, and fighting off illness, one day is taken in by a kind soul. This kind soul gives them warm clothes, feeds them well, nurtures them with love, and offers them a cozy bed to sleep in. Without thinking twice, this child is overwhelmed in gratitude, for she never dreamed that something so special was possible. Her feelings of love and appreciation for her new life are beyond what any child growing up with these common necessities could reach. The child that went without understands what it feels like to be deprived of a home. Now having a home, more love and gratitude is found.

This story illustrates humanity's journey from separation consciousness back into unity consciousness. For such a long time, we have walked upon a road that offers little shelter and nothing close to a comfortable place for rest. Instead, we have been strung out by the stress and the conflict of a dream that is without unity. We have worn ourselves down to the point where we have not only forgotten ourselves. We have forgotten that our neighbors are also a part of us and that when we cause another pain, we are causing ourselves pain. When we lie to another, we are lying to ourselves. When we deceive another, we are deceiving ourselves.

And so we have walked, we have stumbled, crawled, and scrapped our knees in desperation to find our home, only to discover that it was right here all along – in our own heart.

Love is the path of oneness

Giving compassion to yourself, loving yourself, and allowing your heart to open up will allow you to see all of creation in a different light. It will inspire true insight, clarity of vision, and will motivate change in your life that your old self would never have imagined. Your old self was addicted to the stories and justifying the stories. The reason is that they were right and everyone else was wrong. Your new self, which is unified to all of creation, will no longer see through that belief, but rather will witness with intelligence – the intelligence that honors all of creation and the inward and outward flows of its perfect expression.

This space of love does not separate itself from anything, it sees all as its own reflection and honors all as its own life. The individual doesn't separate man from animal or animal from flower; instead, there's perfect honor in it all. The love is so profound that the person senses all of creation and the myriad of feelings that are generated within its expression.

Have you ever watched a movie that you were so captivated by that you found yourself flooded by tears at the end of the movie? You had dived so deeply into the story and the characters, (and even though it was make-believe) you could feel what the characters were feeling. This is a feeling of oneness.

Honoring the story

When an individual is embodying oneness, they don't separate themselves from the world around them and laugh in the face of other people's pain, because "they know" it is just a story. Instead, there is a deep understanding and wisdom that this individual now possesses for they understand the process of life and the journey that each individual is on in order to wake up. This creates a lot of compassion. They have been there, lost in the illusion of the story themselves. More than ever, they see with open eyes and are capable of assisting those surrounding them, helping them remember their own perfect wholeness.

And so the next level of dreaming takes place, which is a very lucid dream that a master plays. This is the act of awakening the dreamer. Like a shaman that weaves himself in and out of realities, he communicates to each and every person, telling them exactly what they need to hear so that they may wake up – fully understanding the complexities of each story and the truth beyond the story.

We are all fragile individuals and the awakening process can be a shock to our system if we are to unravel it all at once. We must be patient and slow, giving love and compassion to every dimension of our perceived self and misunderstood identity.

This works in the same way as if you were told your whole life that the world was flat and then one day someone came to your village and told you the world was round. But, how? That would be the first question you ask. Maybe the person has no real way of telling you and that the only tangible way to be sure is if you hop on the next boat and sail around the globe to see if you find yourself right back where you started in the first place.

See for yourself

This is one boat ride that you cannot miss. It offers you the journey home, and a physical experience of oneness. You can read all the pages in this book but until you decide to put it into practice, you will never truly know. The knowledge will simply be something you read but it will never be anything that you truly know, until you have taken that journey.

On the journey back to oneness, you will have many questions. More and more will rise as you come closer to your authentic self. The reason being is that the more you know yourself, the more questions will arise. The less you know about yourself, the less you care to ask. It is kind of like a teenager who hits adolescence and all of a sudden, thinks he knows more than everyone in the world. Don't be afraid of the questions that live inside of you. They are there to be asked and no one is laughing at you for asking them. If they do, it is only because they fear the question themselves.

You are allowed to know every mystery that has ever existed in the universe. You are allowed to know the reason for every action that has ever occurred on this planet. You should love those who have tried to keep it from you (maybe it was the government, your religion, or the media) because they are you. They are the part of you that is afraid of knowing itself. They are the part of you that is embarrassed or ashamed of their ill deeds. They are the part of you that is just as scared to come out of the darkness. Instead of hunting them down and pointing fingers, give them a hand up. Love them and show them that there is another way to experience life. Be a living example of love and oneness and most of all, be true to yourself. In doing so, you set the world free.

Chapter 13

Heaven on Earth

No matter where what we do, or where we go our individual reality will reflect where our consciousness is. You can be sitting on a tropical island somewhere far away and still be experiencing hell. As we step into the embodiment of oneness, we move into a place of realization that we as individuals are nothing more than a storehouse of information contained in a blanket of consciousness. We realize that all information created in this illusion is in fact an illusion and it is only the certainty you place on the information that makes it a fact. When there's more certainty, there's more strength and conviction in this fact.

We must remember that the world we live in, the science we study, the languages, the cultures, and everything we know to be true is a product of our collective agreement. Yes, we can say that science proves this and science proves that, yet it is us who have formulated a definition surrounding what "this & that" truly is. As we continue to make breakthrough after breakthrough within science, we are starting to realize surprising information and much of these new discoveries point to the infinite self.

All of these studies that we continue to find through science is a reflection of our consciousness. You can often tell a lot about a civilization by their science and math. If we look back to many of the ancient cultures like the Mayans or the Egyptians or even the Greeks, we see that their abilities (when it came to math and science) were far beyond what our current scope can see. These civilizations produced so much proof that our level of western science is merely touching the surface. Long before we had computers, these ancient cultures would commune with the place of unity that connected them to all knowledge. Their ability to open their mind and commune with the greater universe gave them a greater relationship to the knowledge of all things. You can see this with any relationship. The greater the unity, the more information you know about it.

In these ancient cultures, there was no separation between their spirituality and their science. There was a great honor in knowing that they were one, hence the unity consciousness. By allowing ourselves to truly merge in the knowingness of our oneness, all things begin to connect.

You can look to the evidence that many of these civilizations left behind – from their drawings of the star systems, to their architecture and their use of natural resources. With every invention that was ever made in these ancient cultures, there was always one thing in common. It took into account the greater environment and the larger universe. In ancient Indian architecture called Vedic architecture, you can see that, not only were the buildings built with grace and style; there was a math that was based on sacred geometry, which is the true language of the universe. These were then based on degrees, the seasons, alignment with the stars, and the use of all the elements of earth, air, fire, water, and ether, to bring out different energies to balance the whole flow of the home.

A modern day architect would have a lot of studying to do if he was going to build a house in the same way. It could take him a lifetime to understand the essence of creating a home based on all these principles. Since this knowledge was naturally their way of life, these systems were innately built into everything.

Since we are discussing architecture as a mere example of living in unity verses living in separation from unity, let's take a look at the primary focus of houses today. When looking at a house, usually the number one priority is that it is attractive. The next few aspects that one may make into account would be how many bedrooms, bathrooms etc. This is then followed by our individual preferences such as must have sunlight, large kitchen for cooking, backyard, spacious dining area etc. As you can see, the way we see our prospective house are different than that of the ancient cultures. Our preferences either come from the appearance or practicality. As we start to merge ourselves with the greater unity, we may start to see our preferences change or grow.

If we take a look back through time, we see a place where people were more connected to unity. Were they in heaven? We don't know. But obviously something must have happened to make these civilizations fall. What was it that made these civilizations and their great wisdom disappear beneath the ruble? We have continued forward today in search of greater ways to be happy and live in harmony.

Every human being has one calling in life and that is to be in a state of harmony. When we are in harmony, the world around us is in harmony. We have all felt harmony in our lives. Maybe not all the time, but I'm sure we can all reflect and remember feeling harmony flowing through our veins. Maybe we just got a massage, or we were having a beautiful connected conversation with your partner. Perhaps it was a time of feeling really alive and healthy.

Recreating harmony

Think back to a time when you truly felt harmony? Now that you can locate that time, ask yourself the following questions: Where was I when I felt harmony?

What had just occurred?

What did my mind feel like?

What did my emotions feel like?

What did my body feel like?

How did I act towards others, my environment, and the world when I felt harmony?

When we are in a state of harmony, our body, mind, and emotions feel relaxed, open, and free. When we live in harmony with our body, mind, and emotions, we naturally feel a greater connection to the larger environment, its people, and the places around us. This greater connection then creates a deeper understanding. So the decisions we make in the environment and our relationships, and the greater world at large comes from a more unified, compassionate space. Naturally you would imagine that those people who lived in times of harmonious intelligence such as the ones mentioned would have also been in greater harmony with themselves.

When we lose touch with our individual harmony, the decisions we make with those people, the environment, and the greater world become disconnected. Think back to a time when you felt out of harmony. Maybe you were seriously ill, angry with a friend, or facing challenges in life. Once you locate this memory, answer the following questions:

What was happening when I was out of harmony?

What did my mind feel like?

What did my emotions feels like?

What did my body feel like?

How did I act towards others, my environment, and the world when I was out of harmony?

When we are experiencing challenges in life, we feel out of harmony. This propels all of our awareness to shut down as we become the victim to our circumstances. In doing this, we propel our unhealthy and disconnected consciousness into everything we do. This creates a selfish mentality and people begin fighting for resources and competing against each other. That is why in order for us to experience heaven on earth; we must do the necessary steps to change our inner environment, body, mind, and emotions. We must stop blaming other people and start taking responsibility for our individual health as the number one priority.

The reason I would make the recommendation of looking after your individual health first is because when you are healthy, you are more unified to pure consciousness and true intelligence. Once the intelligence is living within every vibrating particle of your consciousness, then the decisions you make and the abilities you have for creating change in the world around you is so much more profound.

Let's look at a situation between a mom and her daughter. Mom, lets call her Janet, is quite insecure and often suffers from anxiety attacks along with a wave of depressive emotions. These unhealthy cycles within her are a result of never being aware of those areas of fear that have traveled with her most her life. Due to this fact, she places a lot of rules and restrictions on her daughter, Lucie, who is now 18 years old. Lucie was born into her family as an adventurous soul, yet because of her mother's constant fears, she has been given very little leeway to live out her dream, which is to work in the Amazon, studying endangered species. This type of job is unrealistic and frightening to Janet. She believes that if she were to allow her child to go to the Amazon, without a phone in the middle of the jungle, with wild animals, she may never see her daughter again. This fear may be quite valid, yet is it valid for Lucie or just Janet?

Lucie is forced to change her career path because of her mother's fears and ends up doing a job that brings her very little satisfaction. In response, Janet feels comfortable in her fears since Lucie is no longer attempting to leave the country on a jungle safari.

This situation happens time and time again. Not only within families but the whole world. The truth is by projecting your insecurities on others, you are forcing them to adapt to your level of disconnection from unity consciousness. Let's move into the field of complete awareness and see that Janet is an enlightened being, who carries with her complete trust and understanding. Would her decision to allow her daughter's trip to the Amazon be the same? Maybe in Janet's high awareness she might recognize the potential dangers, but also since residing in unity. She can assist her daughter in being as aware as she is so that if any challenges came up while in the Amazon, Lucie would be equipped with the awareness to make the right decision for her safety.

When there is awareness, there is no longer fear. Fear has a tendency to lock itself onto the body and create all sorts of disconnection. We only have to look at the current state of the world to see that there is a great lack of unity in our decisions as one world. Perhaps there has been unity within different countries, yet there has not been unity with all the countries working together for the benefit of all. It has turned into a schoolyard fight between resources and toys! This is another result of the disconnection from unity consciousness and an agreement with the illusion.

Your true identity

With the fast movement of today's world, I would say no wonder much of the world is out of touch with heaven on Earth. In addition to the schoolyard fight between countries, we as individuals are racing a million miles a minute in search of a quick pleasure, hoping that perhaps it may resemble a slice of heaven. From fast food chains and pharmaceutical medications to brothels in every red light district, the addiction to quick pleasure or pain relief has the world lost in a boat without a sail. What are we racing for? What are we hoping to achieve by moving so fast? In our addiction to illusion we have somehow convinced ourselves if we move faster we will get to our destination sooner? Yet our only destination is a state of oneness and that's already here. We can fool ourselves by saying that our destination is something different than oneness. We could say that it is material gain, personal success, and pleasures of the outside world or victory in your business endeavors or family life. But if we were to ask ourselves, what does each of these accomplishments make us feel, the answer is that they give us a feeling of oneness. Yet, they don't last forever. Soon, that success will fade and you will have another assignment to drive you forward.

A person can never be completely happy if they are making all these triumphs, their outlet for wholeness. Yes, they will have moments of extreme bliss and celebration, yet the addiction to the outside world will move them in and out of the game, and so the rollercoaster of life will continue with high highs ad low lows.

What if someone told you that you could have more love, joy, happiness and wholeness than you could ever imagine, without all the stress. Perhaps you would not believe me, because you only know what you have been taught, and you can only base your knowledge on what you have experienced. But just because you have not experienced it, does that mean it doesn't exist?

Heaven is a state of consciousness, and it is not dependent on the gains of the outside world. It comes from deep inside the eternal wells of your true nature. It lives inside of you, and with the right tools you can go there whenever you like. You do not need someone to take you there; you do not need any amount of money, any possession or material object to give it to you. You already own it, and you could not throw it away, even if you tried, because it is your true nature. Everything else is transient, your likes and dislikes, your personality, your passions, your dreams, your attachments, your relationships and all your viewpoints. They are all transient. The only thing that remains the same the whole way through is your connection to the oneness, whether you are aware of it or not.

No matter who you are, what your nationality is, what religion you belong to, what cultural beliefs you follow, the underlining intention is the same, we are all seeking oneness, unification with the whole, because this is the greatest state of harmony.

Unwinding the coil

Over the history of time, humanity has experienced countless stories of war, disease, famine, hatred and loss. These stories have perpetuated the larger story of separation and the way we relate to our brothers and sisters on the planet. Each of us have been affected by these stories, not only through our own individual beliefs and perceptions, but through the deep link in our genetics; each individual inheriting the stories through their genetic make-up, thus perpetuating further disease and ailments in the body and thus the continuing the stories that lack harmony and oneness.

Science is now proving that the power of thought and belief are capable of changing the structure of our DNA. This new outlook on our genes gives us back the power to control our own health. Best selling author and scientist Gregg Braden, speaks of this in his book; The Spontaneous Healing of Belief.

In one of his experiments, Gregg Braden placed human DNA into 28 vials and gave each vial to a researcher. Each researcher holding the vial had been trained extensively to generate strong positive and negative emotions. When the researchers felt emotions such as gratitude, love and appreciation the DNA responded by relaxing. The strands unwound themselves, increasing the length of the DNA. When the researchers experienced lower emotions such as anger, fear and frustration the DNA became confined and shortened. What was also found was when the DNA became confined many of the codes inside turned off and when the DNA became relaxed the codes were turned back on.

Humans have become so complex that rather than living in a natural state of harmony, we are wound up like a tight coil and it has become hard for us to simply let go and relax. Even when we think we are relaxed, we are not even close the level of relaxation that can potentially be available to us. This is not our individual fault. It's the result of the generations upon generations that have lived before us and the build up of tension that has been passed down through out the ages and finally, being delivered to us through our beliefs systems and our genetic code.

One example is the way we are conditioned to hold ourselves in social situations. Our programming is usually so deep that we don't even realize we are holding a posture, or expressing ourselves in a way that is presenting a persona that we have been taught is "acceptable". Much of the time we may be presenting a posture yet feeling something different inside. However, since we fear that what we feel inside is "wrong" we present a posture so that the world outside world accepts us. This action alone blocks us from processing the coiled up energy in our system, inhibiting our ability to feel a complete state of harmony and oneness at all times.

Living a simple life

Living a simple and relaxed life should be the easiest thing for us to do, since the Earth provides us all that we need. Yet, humans have built systems that require more attention and maintenance in order for us to feel safe and comfortable. We have created a system that is dependent on money for survival rather than the abundant land and the blessings that come directly from the Earth. We have separated ourselves from the good nature of our community for emotional support and now spend thousands of dollars on psychiatrists, we spend every last penny on our social security rather than create security through love and community, we have boxed ourselves into a family of 5 and expect life to be easy when bringing up our children when it used to take a whole village to bring up a child, we have disconnected from the intelligence of knowing our own bodies and instead we listen to so called "experts" who tell us to put poison in our bodies and we follow. We have stopped listening to our own intuition and now obey the prophecy of the media and we have forgotten to love ourselves, because the world tells us, we are not good enough, skinny enough, successful enough or wealthy enough to be loved.

The world has become lost in the complexity of story and it is time for us to unwind and feel safe enough in our hearts, to trust the process of this unwinding. It may be daunting, but in order for this to take place, we have to open ourselves up to see all that we have hidden from for so long. We must be open to witness all the lies we have told our self, and to face all the actions that ever created guilt within our hearts, toward our self and each other. In the act of doing this, collectively, we are able to realize that no one is to blame and that we have all played our part in creating the stories together. Every single one of us has played a role in separation consciousness and no one is left out. Now it is time for us to wake up, forgive ourselves for forgetting our true nature and choose to live a life that is liberated from illusion.

We are experiencing a time in human history where the lies are being exposed, and we must always remember that those lies, wherever they came from, are a part of our own story as well. So rather than hanging on to them, let us release them into the wind. This way we can remain open to receiving a new life and a new world based on a higher order: An order that is in tune, not only with the natural rhythms of our planet, but also the natural alignment of our greater galaxy and universe. May we be open enough in our consciousness to conceive the possibility of other worlds, other planets and other life forms, while choosing to see in great wonder our own potential, and capabilities as human beings of infinite capacity.

We have waited a long time to reach this point in consciousness. We are the ones that we have been waiting for! We carry the key to creating heaven on Earth, for we have learnt and understood all that is necessary to leave the past behind and to embrace a future of higher qualities. We have experienced every aspect of separation consciousness to know that it is a less enjoyable game to play than the connection and love of oneness.

Trust in your intuition and if the old stories try to creep back in, remember that your life is made for greatness and that love and harmony is your true nature.

Thank you for being patient with others who are also on the road of remembering. It is patience and kindness that allows this shift to touch every corner of the globe. So take your time and feel your heart overflow in joy, because you are already home and there is nothing else left to do other than celebrate this beautiful gift called life!

Welcome home.

About the Author

Jennifer Brooke Partridge is internationally renowned as a spokesperson and facilitator in the human potentiality fields. She has spent time studying ancient texts that point to the process of awakening, while traveling to remote monasteries and sacred sites across the globe, and learning from various ancient cultures and traditions. She is an Ashtanga and Kundalini yoga teacher and intuitive guide working with many sacred healing arts from shamanic healing, Ayurveda, Reiki, Massage, Mantras, Earth Medicines, Yoga, Chanting and so much more. She has devoted her life to her spiritual practice and sharing the message of personal evolution through her career as a journalist, researcher and spokesperson.

Jennifer graduated from Perth, Western Australia's T.A.F.E College in Broadcast Presentation in 2001. Since this time she has appeared in an array of radio, television and film projects. In 2007, Jennifer moved from Australia to U.S.A. In this time she launched her media Production Company titled Our New Earth Productions. In O.N.E productions Jennifer has scripted, hosted and produced radio, TV, online and film content.

In her career, Jennifer has had the opportunity of working with the industries best in motivation, spirituality and health. Interviewing visionaries such as Gregg Braden, don Miguel Ruiz, William from The Black Eyed Peas, Michael Beckwith, David Wolfe, and Shiva Rea amongst many others. She has travelled extensively on film projects and research assignments to places such as India, Nepal, Bali, Thailand, Colombia, Costa Rica, Korea, Singapore, Mexico, North America and Australia. She has been working in radio actively for over 9 years, hosting currently hosting her own program on KCSB 91.9fm Santa Barbara. In addition she is featured as a host on shows such as Living Foods, on Oasis TV.

Jennifer has been discussing expanded states of consciousness and awakening in popular documentaries such as "The Voice," her recent T.V. series pilot "Wisdom of the World" and books such as "Dream, Awake" and "America without Money". She also loves to travel the world, sharing her inspiration at festivals, conferences and public gatherings.

For more information on Jennifer, you can reach her through her various web platforms:

www.ournewearth.tv

www.jenniferbrookepartridge.com

Jennifer is available for bookings, appearances and teachings globally and can be reached at info@ournewearth.tv for further details.